TOM JACKSON AND ELLEN JACKSON

PERFECT RESUME STRATEGIES

75 Success Stories of Real People in Times of Change— the resumes, cover letters, and strategies they used

DOUBLEDAY

NEW YORK LONDON TORONTO SYDNEY AUCKLAND

Dedication

This book, and the affection and love of the authors, is dedicated to the full body of career counselors—now worldwide—who spend their days contributing to the worklives of others. This professional cadre of helping and caring people stretches from the public sector JTPA counselor, to the college placement center director, to the private-executive-level outplacement coach. We know and admire the quality of personal commitment and attention their work requires, and acknowledge those who have made it their passion.

Acknowledgments

To the seventy-five anonymous people whose career stories, resumes and cover letter samples make up the major body of this book.

To the twenty-nine career counselor/advisors who contributed the stories and sample resumes: Carol Allen, Jack and Phoebe Ballard, Judy Kaplan Baron, Joyce Cohen, Patricia Dietze, Barbara Kabcenell Ellman, Bonnie Traylor-FitzSimmons, Monika Freidel, Pam Gross, Betsy Jaffe, Eileen Javers, Mike Kenney, Clemm Kessler, Kathy Kouzmanoff, John Mattson, Ken McCoy, Patricia O'Keefe, William O'Toole, Phyllis Harper Rispoli, Carl Schneider, Jane Shuman, Peggy Simonsen, Alexine Smith, Jerry Sturman, Minh-Nhat Tran, Melvyn and Sharon Tuggle, and Bill Young.

To Roberta Harper, who faithfully gathered early material, typed it and kept it organized, and to Susan Ray for editorial help.

To Megan Denver who took the final draft materials to completion and turned the computer into a servant, not a master.

To John Duff, our Doubleday "Perfect" editor, patient to the end.

Thank you. Nothing worthwhile is ever done alone.

—Tom Jackson and Ellen Jackson
Woodstock, New York 1992

PUBLISHED BY DOUBLEDAY
a division of Bantam Doubleday Dell Publishing Group, Inc. 666 Fifth Avenue, New York, New York 10103
DOUBLEDAY and the portrayal of an anchor with a dolphin are registered trademarks of Doubleday, a division of Bantam Doubleday Dell Publishing Group, Inc. Library of Congress Cataloging-in-Publication Data

Jackson, Tom.
Perfect resume strategies : 75 success stories of real people in times of change—the resumes, cover letters, and strategies they used / by Tom Jackson and Ellen Jackson. — 1st ed.
p.   cm.
Companion volume to The perfect resume. c1990. Includes index.
1. Resumes (Employment) 2. Applications for positions. I. Jackson, Ellen (Ellen Perry) II., Title. HF5383.J26 1992
650.14—dc20
91-45480
CIP

ISBN 0-385-18112-4

1 3 5 7 9 10 8 6 4 2

FIRST EDITION

Table of Contents

Introduction: How to Get the Most from This Book.

Most resume books, no matter how perfect, take a generalized approach to the construction of this most important self-marketing document: Explore your inner skills, focus on a job target, select the right format, load up with action verbs . . . ready, set, write!

This book looks more deeply into the soul of the job search, as well as the job searcher. This is a book about people who came face-to-face with a changed reality in their lives—a slip in their career plan—which made them change from a generalized approach to their career future to some very specific strategies designed to move them beyond a particular predicament or challenge. They had to undertake a transition from an old view of their future to a new way of seeing it in the context of a dynamic changing workplace.

In the upcoming pages you will take a short journey into people's lives. You will feel the challenges they faced, and learn how they managed to refocus themselves for the future. You will see courage in action. You will learn how, through productive interactions with coaches or counselors, people were able to reframe the structure of their careers and initiate course corrections that would propel them in new directions. You will experience some of their surprise and discovery. And you will learn something about the human spirit as it relates to the workaday world. You will watch people taking charge of their lives while avoiding hazardous cubbyholes and stultifying slots.

Today's economy does not provide an ideal marketplace for careers as we have defined them for 50 or more years. We no longer have a predictable future. This book is about intention moving beyond prediction: an assertive, creative mind pointing forward to something fresh and new, and the will to take action in these new directions and dimensions.

Read this book with an eye to the process as well as the ultimate product—the resume. Every story is relevant in terms of the strategies used to redirect, refocus, or rebuild a future. One person's move from teaching to business consulting might demand the same kind of transformation as another person's move from public sector accounting to private investment portfolio managing.

THE STRATEGIC APPROACH

Today's job market is highly complex. Organizational needs, marketplaces, technology and the shifting sands of a dynamic global economy leave us on edge, having to shift from security to versatility in the management of our future worklives. Without a constructive and thoughtful use of strategy, you are likely to find yourself stranded in the backwaters of the economy. To move forward and upward in a logical, straightforward way will probably not gain the most ground in your personal career development. Rather, you will need to respond to the challenge the way a surfer would: Adapt your movements to the demands of the wave patterns. Use change to your advantage.

Strategy and career entrepreneurship are woven throughout the success stories on these pages. People have organized their skills, abilities, and accomplishments in their resumes so that they focus on future needs and desires, emphasizing their ability to solve problems and add value, rather than simply posturing through their past job titles and positions. People in this book are repositioning, not reinventing. We propose that you escape the tyranny of a restrictive job title and describe yourself in terms of your capability and capacity for generating value in future assignments. It is this versatility that is a key factor for future-minded job seekers.

The people in these stories are examining the quality of life. We go through the paces with many people who discovered that their programmed directions were either impossible to follow or boring, repetitive, and demeaning. Rather than resign themselves to long journeys into oblivion, these people interacted with powerful career counselors and refocused their worklives in a way that would be inherently more satisfying, rewarding, and life-enhancing.

THE CAREER COACH

It is very hard to make substantial changes in life direction on your own. Because of our tendency to box ourselves into old assumptions, roles, and self-fulfilling prophecies, often we find ourselves struggling against unseen boundaries. With our dreams deflated we come to the conclusion that we can't make the change; we're too old, too young, or too broke to take charge of our lives. The job of the career counselor or coach is to take you outside of yourself, to dissolve the entrapment of your current view of the situation, and open you up to a new world of possibility. Good career coaches treat you as fully workable. When you are down on yourself, they are up on you. The twenty-nine high-performing career coaches who contributed to this book are committed to the expansion of people's workability and worklives— the enhancement of self-expression to reach ends that are honorable, productive, and alive. If you have a perplexing or snagging predicament and need to move out of old trajectories into new ones, you need a coach. This could be a professional career counselor, a member of the staff of a college or secondary school, or a friend who knows the rules of the road and is not afraid to push you beyond your own self-limitations. As you read the success stories in this book, you will see how the guidance of the career coach made all the difference in the quality of people's worklives, and frequently moved them into better jobs faster.

However, remember this: a career coach or counselor is not a placement agent. It is not his or her job to move you quickly into an opening somewhere and stamp the file "closed." The role of a career coach or counselor is to empower you to make the decisions that are crucial to your own future; to help you position your resume, and design a marketing campaign and an effective career strategy; and to coach you along the way. The relationship with a career coach is much like the relationship with a mentor: empowering, truthful, and consistent.

This is a book about real people and real situations. The identities, and some facts about the career candidates and their situations, have been changed for reasons of personal privacy; however, the situational reality is intact. The professional counselors and consultants who helped engineer these strategies are real.

We unashamedly recommend the twenty-nine people who have contributed to the success of the vignettes portrayed herein. Their names and addresses appear at the end of this book. If working with any of them is not convenient for you, we suggest that you reach out in your own community— ask for recommendations, check with the local university or high school, and finally, if no leads are present, check under "career services" in the classified directories. Before establishing a relationship with a career consultant who has not been recommended to you, we suggest an introductory meeting of fifteen to twenty minutes in which you and the career consultant discuss how he or she will work, what period of time will be entailed, and what the fees will be. It is not necessary to make a deal on the first meeting and we recommend that you interview two or three to get the person who will be most appropriate to your needs.

Part One

Strategies for Success

The key principles for approaching a strategic resume and marketing communication.

BREAKING OUT OF BOXES

In the job market of the nineties, it is imperative to take stock of where you stand. It is a mistake to simply continue moving in a routine career direction without stopping to ask some key questions about your worklife assumptions. We're not saying that a straight-line approach isn't the one you should take, but simply that before you write another chapter in the same novel, you reconsider the plot, characters, and setting. Take a few days to ask yourself some deep questions about the direction of your career. Is it satisfying and energizing? Is it practical? Does it have a future? If it even exists into the twenty-first century, will it still have meaning then for you?

It is helpful to have someone else interact with you in examining how you put together your future work model. It is useful to step outside the security blanket of the payroll, benefits, and perks of the job to make sure you have examined the internal payoffs: satisfaction, personal growth, contribution to society, onward and upward learning.

When you challenge the current view of your situation, you are open to a limitless variety of possibilities. Read periodicals and current publications in your desired field and talk to others to brainstorm career directions that will enhance your personal stake. You may find your current career direction is very satisfying. However, there could be a need to reconsider your marketing approach, to look for fresh new ways of presenting yourself that are better directed toward future needs than past accomplishments.

The Strategic Marketing Communication

The way you get the job you want is to communicate about yourself in a way that provokes interest and desire to a potential employer or customer. It is crucial to present yourself in a way that resonates with the needs of any given employer representative, recruiter, or manager. For many of us, the strategic approach directed to these needs will be a major change in style. Traditionally, we have been trained to present ourselves as a series of chronologies: where we were, what we did, what we were called, and so on. Considering the demands of the future job market, it is clear that this is no longer sufficient. What we have done in the past may not be needed in the same way in the future. The rate of change of job descriptions and positions is substantial. Simply positioning yourself as doing more of what you've already done will fail to gain you the maximum competitive advantage.

In this book we deal with two major parts of the strategic marketing communication—the resume and the cover letter (also called the marketing letter). These two must work together. A good resume is essential and this book will show you how to put together the best.

However, a resume gets a particular kind of reading. Even when it is well organized and well focused it tends to be cold and impersonal. For the most part, it talks about you and your problem-solving capabilities in a general way. The strategic marketing letter (or cover letter), on the other hand, is personal in nature. It is directed to a particular person and delivers a compelling message to that person. It takes the reader through the process of determining how you will meet the need in *that* job. A good cover letter stimulates the interest of the employer to get the facts from your resume. Working together in partnership, the perfect resume and the perfect cover letter will open up doors and establish relationships that can lead to a prosperous career future.

The Resume

A powerful resume is your best advertisement for self-marketing. In its one- or two-page layout (preferably one-page) it presents a forward-looking story of your capabilities and their relevance to a future worklife. Its very presentation—neat, organized, clear, effective, and well spoken—demonstrates how you will get the job done.

A perfect resume is usually presented in one of several conventional or traditional formats. However, as this book will show you, there is room for versatility. It is essential to choose a structure that enables the information to be presented in a clear and easy-to-understand way, but don't let form interfere with function. Don't let the rigidity of any resume format keep you from fully expressing what you want the employers to hear. In reviewing the resume examples observe how the words and phrases are positioned to direct the reader to the benefit and payoff. Examine the layouts to see how attractive they are to the eye. Look at the economy of wording. Notice how the most relevant information is at the beginning of the resume and then substantiated or supported. For further guidance turn to the resume-writing rules in Part Three of this book; or, for a complete guide to putting together a powerful resume from scratch, get a copy of *The Perfect Resume* by this same author and publisher. (See Resources, page 202.)

RESUME-WRITING RULES: CONDENSED VERSION

Know the employer and the employer's needs.   Focus the resume so that it describes benefits and accomplishments, not simply jobs and duties.

Customize your resumes.   Do this for each major job target—not necessarily each employer (your cover letter will do that). If you have several career directions make sure that you're not trying to use one resume to handle them all. Using a good word processor or *The Perfect Resume Computer Kit* (see Resources, page 202) will assist you in doing this effectively.

Select the format that works best for you.   There are three basic formats, plus a number of combination formats that you will see throughout the "success stories" in Part Two of this book. Briefly, they are:

- Chronological Resume: This resume format organizes your information in chronological order, starting with the most recent experience and moving back to earlier experiences.

- Functional Resume: This resume format organizes your experience into functional categories (design, research, sales, etc.). By organizing the information in a functional category, you can bring to the forefront of your resume the functions that are most relevant to where you're heading in the future. This avoids the difficulty that often occurs when your current or most recent job is not the one you want in the future.

- Targeted Resume: Normally (although there are many exceptions in this book) we don't recommend having a career objective or job target on the resume itself. We prefer to have this in the marketing communication or cover letter. The exception to this is the targeted resume. This resume is designed for one particular job opening. Along with a strategic marketing letter, it points to something in a particular employment situation. The resume starts with the candidate's capabilities ("I can" statements), and emphasizes what he or she can do in the future. This section is followed by the candidate's accomplishments, which show what he or she has done in the past.

- Combination Resume: There are many creative ways of combining the targeted, functional, and chronological approaches. In reviewing the examples in this book remember that you have some flexibility in how to put your resume together.

Eliminate extraneous information.   Potential employers don't need to know your social security number, references from prior employers, height, weight, vital statistics, and the like. Remember that during the employment process there will be an application and more details can be provided then.

Edit carefully.   We mean it. Get someone else who understands English usage, spelling, and grammar to scrutinize the resume and look for ways that it can be upgraded.

Make it beautiful.   Spend some time, and if necessary get some help here, to get the layout clean, crisp, and easy to read. Don't overdo the use of boldface and underlining and fancy type. Do use good margins and lots of white space so that the brilliance of what you say stands out on the page.

THE STRATEGIC MARKETING (COVER) LETTER

The cover letter puts you in the driver's seat. It allows you to adjust your communication to the needs of each and every particular employer to whom you are sending your resume. By using the cover letter effectively, customizing it all the way and using a word processor or computer package such as *The Strategic Letter Writer* (see Resources, page 202), you will be able to quickly and easily generate individualized, customized cover letters for each prospective employer. Employers receive mailsacks full of resumes and form letters for their most attractive job openings. The lack of finesse in these communications often leaves the readers bored and unresponsive. By creating a powerfully focused presentation package you can stimulate interest, revive the awareness of the employer, and get yourself invited in for interviews.

RULES FOR EFFECTIVE MARKETING COMMUNICATION OR COVER LETTER

Know what you want.   Keep in mind your preferred type of job, location, size of company, and type of organization. Clearly targeting what you want makes it easier to send your resume and cover letter to the appropriate person. Avoid mass mailings.

Know or project what the employer needs or wants.   If you were the employer, what would you be looking for? The more you learn in advance the more you are able to make your marketing communication mean something to the employer. Do library research, talk to people, stay in touch with the marketplace. If you don't know enough about a specific employer, extrapolate from the needs of the industry or economy as a whole.

Know what you have to offer.   Select accomplishments, capabilities, and training from your background that will relate to the future needs of the employer. You don't need to advertise only what you've done. You can express what you *can do* in a more targeted approach; your capability to accomplish can go before your proven track record, if necessary.

Create interest in your presentation. Express something early on that shows you know what the employer is about. This could be a problem, a situation, or an opportunity that speaks to the employer in his or her language.

Direct the letter to a particular person by name. Do not use "Dear Sir/Madame," or another generalized salutation. By getting the name of the person to whom you are writing, you will increase the interest from the other end immediately.

Don't say too much. Include just enough information to direct the employer to investigate the benefits of what you are proposing.

Speak in the language of benefit. Don't speak of how hard you're going to work or how much education you have. Focus your communications in a way that the person hiring you sees the result that he or she can expect.

Keep sentences and paragraphs short. Keep your letter easy to scan, reread, and comprehend.

Make a beautiful product. Send a well-typed, clear, attractive presentation, with impeccable spelling and grammar.

Have an effective closing. Suggest the next action you want to see happen—a meeting or phone call, a decision to talk further. Mention that you will call for a meeting.

Keep records. Maintain a log of the letters and resumes you send out so you can follow up easily on them at preappointed times.

Part Two

Success Stories

*Seventy-five stories of real people in times of change—
the resumes, cover letters, and strategies
they used to achieve their employment goals.*

REAL PEOPLE

As we have watched the working world rapidly become more spontaneous and unpredictable we have recognized the necessity to expand the approach of our popular book *The Perfect Resume*, and to present a broader range of ideas about how resumes and cover letters can be used in a complex job market. What started as an idea for a catalogue developed into this collection of case histories of people confronting challenging job change situations, including a description of the predicament in which each person found him- or herself, the strategy used to address the predicament, and samples of the actual resumes and covering letters developed to meet the situation.

To aid us in this endeavor we contacted several dozen well-known career counselors and consultants and asked them to share some of their most interesting recent case histories. We were particularly interested in people who were confronting change in their work situations due to external forces. Out of the hundreds of sets of materials received, we selected seventy-five samples from twenty-nine counselors. These stories are presented here.

Today the Western world is awash in people who are experiencing some level of career predicament. From the basic uncertainty of "Who might buy out my company in the next few years?" to the stressful "My job was eliminated—how do I pay my child's tuition over the next six months *and* find a new job?"—the stories of the people in the following 150 pages represent common threads of late twentieth-century career unease. Given the social, political, technological, and economic forces now in convergence, there is no longer a plain vanilla approach to job finding. In fact, the job search today often represents a challenge of imagination, intelligence, and fortitude.

This book, therefore, goes beyond the simple idea of how to put together a powerful resume to how to construct a complete, custom-tailored communications strategy. What you will see in the following case histories is the combination of a challenge, a process of exploration and strategy—aided by a professional counselor—and the resulting marketing or cover letter and resume. In addition to reviewing final documents that are relevant to your own job search, we recommend that you study as many of the cases as possible to gain insight into the strategic thinking process that went on. There is something of value to be learned in every story.

How to Read the Resumes

In the perfect world, resumes are consistent, well formatted, and logical. What you'll see in the samples that follow will often not match up to these criteria. These are what might be called situational resumes: documents focused for an occasion.

Some of the "rules" we make and break are described in the following paragraphs.

Career Objectives

Generally, we don't recommend including career objectives in a resume. In our opinion they are rarely clear or specific enough to make an impact; and if they *are* quite specific, we think that it narrows the resume. For example, if the candidate states, "Objective: *A middle management position in a Fortune 100 manufacturing company where I can utilize my proven management skills,*" does this mean the candidate won't talk to the subsidiary firm that is only in the Fortune 500? And will that job seeker remember to change that career objective on his or her computer disc when applying for a job in education?

We have rewritten many of the general career objectives on the resumes included in this book to reflect a specific job target.

Qualifications Summaries

Many candidates and counselors like to have a summary paragraph at the top of the resume. We don't believe in it, and think this information belongs in the cover letter, focused on a real job possibility. Only a few summaries made it through our editing process. As you read them you can make the best decision as to whether this should be part of your own approach.

"References Available Upon Request"

Time and again this line keeps popping up on otherwise perfect resumes. We think it is extraneous. Most employers don't assume you come without references.

Two Pages

We are outvoted, and yet unrepentant, in our assertion that a perfect resume should be limited to one page (plus a powerful cover letter). We make our case for this principle elsewhere in the book, and more abundantly in our "mother ship" *The Perfect Resume*. Two-page resumes make up approximately 40 to 45 percent of the samples in this book. We make no apologies for the two-page resumes; as a matter of fact, we think that they work very well—especially when the length supports the major premise of the job-finding strategy.

You'll notice that many resumes are on one page with a reduced typeface. Given the marvelously diverse graphic designs one can now achieve on a good word processor, it has become easier to bring a resume to one page without sacrificing readability.

We have taken the liberty, with the two-page resumes, of having the second page floating behind. Don't worry—once you understand the process, you'll know how to finish your own second page if you really need one.

True Stories

The core issues in the Employment Situations section of each two-page spread are true—exactly as reported by the submitter. The Strategies for Success section also represents what was reported to us. We were not always given the full details of a case; many counselors were extremely protective (and rightly so) of their clients. In some cases we exercised the option that many case history writers use—to prepare an occasional compendium of facts and solutions from people caught up in a similar career dilemma.

Anonymity

We have gone to great lengths to shield the identities of the people whose stories are the core of this book. We've changed names, addresses, company names (with two or three exceptions), colleges, publications, memberships, and so on. If you recognize anyone, it will probably be yourself.

GLOSSARY OF CAREER COUNSELING TERMS

The following alphabetized definitions might be helpful as you read some of the comments about people's careers and their strategies.

CAREER COUNSELORS/CONSULTANTS

Career counselors teach and coach individuals and sometimes groups in job-finding and/or career-enhancement techniques and strategies. Some have Ph.D.'s or master's degrees; many are licensed—and some are effective even without a stack of credentials. Frequently career counselors have both a private practice and a consultation arrangement with organizations who are downsizing and in need of outplacement.

DOWNSIZING OR JOB ELIMINATION

This is the effect of an organization's decision to reduce staff by a significant number of people due to business contraction or internal difficulty.

EXECUTIVE SEARCH RECRUITERS

An executive search agency is retained by an organization to locate and interview people for key positions in the firm. Their work is usually initiated by the hiring organization, and they are frequently paid whether or not they locate the candidate. They provide few if any individually initiated services. An employment agency provides the same function; however, they are more open to individuals who are looking for jobs. They usually get paid based on a placement fee that is earned only when a person is hired.

THE HIDDEN JOB MARKET

The hidden job market represents the vast reservoir of job opportunity that is not advertised. It is usually conveyed by word of mouth or by referral, or represented by unsolved problems that have not yet matured into specific job openings.

INFORMATION INTERVIEW

An information interview is a meeting with anyone who can give you specific, useful information about a specific job field. It is a businesslike approach to gaining information and insight about the field you have chosen to pursue.

Involuntary Furlough

This is a layoff or staff reduction usually for a temporary or indeterminate period of time.

Job Target

A job target is a clearly articulated and committed work direction that has components of personal interest and skill. You may have more than one job target.

Networking

Networking is the process of maintaining an active data base of people who can provide you with introductions, leads, information, and advice. Your network is made up of people who know people who know people. The formation of a network is an essential part of the process of marketing yourself. A network is formed from people you know, even slightly— a former college professor of yours, your attorney, or the mother of your daughter's best friend.

Outplacement

Outplacement refers to the job-search support services provided to individuals by an organization that is downsizing or eliminating jobs.

Self-marketing

Self-marketing is a job-seeking strategy based on the idea that people who want the best job opportunities for themselves will undertake their own aggressive job search rather than wait for an agency, school, or other institution to do it for them. Using a career counselor or coach rather than depending on a placement agency is a good way to supplement a self-marketing campaign.

INDICES

We suggest you read every resume. However, the following indices cover three viewpoints: *situational*, *transitional*, and *job titles* or *functions*. As all seventy-five resumes are arranged alphabetically, we've deleted page number referencing.

SITUATIONAL INDEX

New graduates with little or no substantive work history and/or few marketable accomplishments:

Fitch	Harrington	LaFarge
Frank	Howland	Taylor
Green	Kohl	Wolfson

Women reentering the job market after five or more years as homemakers:

Downes	Foley	Manuel
Fischer	Krebs	

Education/training different from others competing in the same job field:

Albright	Green	McLaughlin
Braunstein	Healy	Misasi
Bridges	Jackson	Randall
Erdos	Kohl	Smithers
Foley	Lane	Tulley
Glassman	Leahy	

Unexpected Job Loss:

Emmans	Logan
Flanders	Mannese
Foltz (merger)	Minnetto
Kelley	Weiss (merger)
Kitsos (merger)	Wisneski
Koch	Witiuk

A history of layoffs—typical of certain industries:

Wisneski

Leaving a "nest" job or career ladder for independent consulting:

Ewing	Landers
Glover	Winters

Starting a business for the first time:

Carroll   Ewing

Returning to an earlier skill or job category after many years in a different job slot:

Albright   Ubell
Erdos   Wilson

Wanting a downgraded position—overqualified for what is currently being sought:

Bartel   McGrory

Steady, logical work history and then a long gap of unemployment with a history of make-do jobs

Albright   Wilson
Bartel

College graduate with a great degree but minimal directly related experience:

Frank   Harrington

Wanting an upgraded position but without obvious or direct experience or skills training for it:

Glassman   Randall
Jackson   Tulley
Kohl

People who are over fifty:

Angelo   Krebs
Carmichael   Lansing
Erdos   Logan
Foley   Mannese
Kitsos   Winters

Mixed work history and education—career gaps due to full-time education:

Holsapple

Living in a town or region where an industry is depressed and all accomplishments and education were connected to that industry:

Kelley   Tulley
Mannese   Wisneski

Great professional career growth and long work history with a single company:

Foltz	Mannese
Garcia	McDonald
Kitsos	Misasi
Koch	O'Connell
Lansing	Tulley

Independent artist/craftsperson with no long-term employer to show specific growth:

Howland	Mulligan

Self-employed representative/consultant/contractor:

Bridges	Holsapple
Foster	Randall
Glassman	Winters

Combined history—worked for others, owned a small business or consultancy, then went back to work for others:

Erdos	Randall
Holsapple	

Short work history: one job (less than five years) and/or one title with diversified assignments:

Kohl	Wolfson
Latham	

Nurse/teacher with job-specific experience:

Downes	Potter

Radical career change with need to overcome heavy biases, such as moving from government work to industry, teaching to business, fine arts to business:

Angelo	Grant
Carmichael	McLaughlin
Crabtree	Smithers
Erdos	Ubell

Internal promotion wanted:

Lane	Widman
Miller	

Handicap/Illness

Harrington	Mantis
Kent	

Miscellaneous

Baretta	Maddan
Corsa	Mantis
Cusack	McGrory
Emmans	O'Connell
Ferguson	Peterson
Garcia	Petruzzo
Lacek	Westerman

TRANSITIONAL INDEX

The following is an index to the resume samples by approximate job category. In many cases people did not change job functions, but did change the industry in which they worked.

	From	To
Albright	Teacher	Corporate Trainer
Angelo	Policeman	Property Manager
Baretta	Organizational Consultant	Organizational Consultant
Bartel	Business Owner	Corporate Manager
Braunstein	Human Resource Generalist	Benefits Administrator
Bridges	Couple—2 careers	Co-Owners (Bed-and-Breakfast)
Carmichael	Service Manager (retired)	Hotel Concierge
Carroll	Corporate Executive	Independent Business Owner
Corsa	Executive Administrator	Same (relocation)
Crabtree	Pharmacist	Corporate Manager
Cusack	Management Consultant	Same (new industry)
Downes	Homemaker/Volunteer	Teacher (returning)
Emmans	Human Resources Director	Same (returning to old industry)
Erdos	Small Business Owner	Non-Profit Administrator
Ewing	Executive (retired 3 years)	Consultant
Ferguson	Senior Executive	Senior Executive
Fischer	Volunteer	Social Services Administrator
Fitch	Military	International Business Relations

From		To
Flanders	Plant Manager	Plant Manager
Foley	Volunteer (part-time paid)	Non-Profit Fund Raiser
Foltz	Senior Manufacturing Manager	Senior Manufacturing Manager
Foster	Entrepreneur (18 years)	Corporate Middle Manager
Frank	New Graduate	Film Production Assistant
Garcia	National Merchandise Manager	International Merchandise Manager
Glassman	Self-Employed (10 years)	Corporate Sales
Glover	Public Sector Adminis- trator	Private Financial Investor
Grant	Teacher/Consultant	Film Producer
Green	New Graduate (Music Major)	Sports Broadcaster
Harrington	New Graduate (Political Science Major)	Social Services Adminis- trator
Healy	Public Relations Writer	Therapist
Holsapple	Independent Therapist	Institutional Therapist
Howland	Classical Musician	Choral Conductor
Jackson	Warehouse Coordinator	Financial Aid Advisor
Kelley	Banking Executive	Banking Executive
Kent	Real Estate Investor	Real Estate Employee
Kitsos	Senior Executive	Senior Executive
Koch	General Manager—Small Retail	General Manager—Small Retail
Kohl	Truck Operations Coordi- nator	Materials Management Trainee
Krebs	Teacher	Health Care Administrator
Lacek	Family-Owned Beauty Business	Cosmetic Firm Manager
LaFarge	New Graduate/Tennis Instructor	High School Spanish Teacher
Landers	Senior Executive (Education)	Corporate Training
Lane	Internal Service Represen- tative (Telecommunica- tions)	Internal Corporate Trainer
Lansing	Executive Manager—Retail	Executive Manager—Retail
Latham	Recent Graduate/ Junior Executive	Recent Graduate/ Junior Executive
Leahy	Multiple Careers (unrelated)	University Teacher
Logan	Full-time Software Engineer	Temporary Consulting Engineer
Maddan	Internal Public Relations	Same Job (raise)

From		To
Mannese	Printed Circuit Designer	Consultant Designer
Mantis	Self-Employed Counselor	Nursing Home Counselor
Manuel	Restaurant Manager	Hotel Administrator
McDonald	Theater Manager (building)	Property Manager
McGrory	Plant Manager	Same (new culture)
McLaughlin	Accountant	Salesperson
Miller	Internal Account Executive	Internal Product Manager
Minnetto	Manager—Equipment Company	Facilities Planner
Misasi	Quality Assurance	Industrial Trainer
Mulligan	University Research Clerk	Events Planner
O'Connell	Corporate Manager	Same (new culture)
Peterson	Corporate Consultant	Corporate Senior Manager
Petruzzo	Detective Investigator	Detective Supervisor
Potter	Parochial School Teacher	Public School Teacher
Randall	Private Practice Counselor	Community Relations Consultant
Smithers	Junior Manager (retail)	Insurance Claims Examiner
Taylor	Dancer/Musician/Actress	Regional Theater Apprentice
Tulley	Marketing Manager (electrical)	Same (electronics)
Ubell	Buyer (electronics)	Community Arts Director
Weiss	Tax Lawyer	Tax Lawyer
Westerman	Domestic Lawyer	Corporate Lawyer
Widman	Administrative Supervisor	Manager
Wilson	Receptionist	Marketing Representative
Winters	Substitute Teacher	Business Consultant
Wisneski	Maintenance Mechanic	Maintenance Mechanic
Witiuk	Sales Administrator	Sales Administrator
Wolfson	News Journalist	Political Journalist

JOB TITLE/FUNCTIONAL INDEX

The following is an index to the resume samples by job title or function.

Administrative Assistant
Harrington

Administrator
Braunstein
Corsa
Erdos
Fischer
Krebs

Attorney
Westerman

Concierge/Hotel Services
Bridges
Carmichael
Manuel

Consultant/Advisor/ Training
Albright
Baretta
Carroll
Fitch
Jackson
Landers
Lane
Logan
Minnetto
Misasi
Mulligan
Randall

Detective
Petruzzo

Electronics/Mechanic
Mannese
Wisneski

Financial
Glover
Weiss

Journalism
Wolfson

Middle Management
Angelo
Bartel
Crabtree
Cusack
Foltz
Koch
Kohl
McLaughlin
Minnetto
Smithers
Widman
Wilson
Witiuk

Musician
Howland
Taylor (dancer)

Public Relations
Lacek
Maddan

Retired
Ewing
Winters

Sales
Foley
Garcia
Glassman
Kent
Latham

Self-Employed
Ewing
Glassman

Senior Management
Emmans
Ferguson
Flanders
Foster
Kelley
Kitsos
Lansing
McDonald
McGrory
Miller
O'Connell
Peterson
Tulley
Ubell

Teacher
Downes
LaFarge
Leahy
Potter

Television/Film Production
Frank
Grant
Green
Leahy

Therapist/Counselor
Fischer
Healy
Holsapple
Mantis

The Case Histories

EMPLOYMENT SITUATION:

Jon left a teaching position in a small Baptist school, unable to support his family of six on so small a salary. Subsequently he made a series of poor career decisions resulting in a number of positions paying only minimum wage, which he supplemented with part-time computer programming.

STRATEGIES FOR SUCCESS:

When Jon first came for counseling, with a limited view of his skills and abilities, he did not acknowledge his computer skills nor did he include them in his resume. Since he had not acquired them through formal training, he assumed they were not legitimately marketable.

His counselor saw two strengths in Jon: his skill with computers and his love of teaching. He and Jon identified positions in which these particular talents could be better utilized; they developed a resume and cover letter that emphasized both his computer and training skills, and integrated his experience as a schoolteacher.

COVER LETTER STATEMENTS:

I am a trainer and teacher who can motivate others to work at their full potential. I am particularly adept with computers and teaching others in their use. For twelve years I enjoyed a successful career in elementary and secondary education. Those years were personally rewarding and professionally productive, but not financially satisfying. I left education to explore other options. In each instance, the most enjoyable aspect of a position turned out to be my opportunity to train and instruct others.

CRITICAL VIEWPOINT:

In the process of networking, Jon received a job offer to teach in an affluent, private non-denominational school with a substantial salary increase and free tuition for his children. After considerable deliberation he accepted the offer, deciding it would put his career back on track and serve as a solid base from which to move toward his new career goal.

We've included his business cover letter, even though Jon ended up back in education. He clearly considered himself worth more money as a result of his detour into business and computers.

Jonathan T. Albright
1630 Cottonwood Drive
Montgomery, AL 36109
(205) 555-4057 (H)
(205) 555-2712 (O)

Objective: **TRAINING SPECIALIST** for a Corporate Training Program

PROGRAMMING/COMPUTER SERVICES
- Wrote program that scored, analyzed, and formulated a report for respondents' answers to a pre-employment test. Resulted in a $100,000 contract.
- Developed a program for pricing, invoicing, and filing that reduced the daily amount of time required for these tasks from 12 hours to 30 minutes.
- Created programs to score tests, monitor student progress, and print report cards. Used by all school personnel.
- Wrote a variety of accounting, check writing, payroll, general ledger, pricing, and data base programs and applications using Basic, Lotus 1-2-3, D base III, and Profile 3.

SUPERVISION/TRAINING
- Supervised and trained 96 guards with Simon's in basic security.
- Responsibilities included scheduling, payroll, organizing new posts, and developing operations manuals for the new posts.
- Developed operating procedures and manual; trained and supervised staff for employment security agency.
- Provided documentation, instructional material, and staff training for the computer applications I have developed.

TEACHING
- Created an academic "monetary" motivation system and simulation exercises which increased average student performance 1.5 years on a nationally normed achievement test.
- Individualized the curriculum for a class of 45 high school students.
- Initiated a creative writing class; conducted literacy training for young adults.
- Taught in an adult education program for two years.

CAREER HISTORY

Programmer	SELF-EMPLOYED	Montgomery, AL	1988 - present.
Scale Operator	CONRAD'S MATERIAL HANDLING	Montgomery, AL	1989 - present.
Captain	SIMON'S SECURITY	Birmingham, AL	1988 - 1989.
Operations Manager	MARITIME SECURITY	Birmingham, AL	1983 - 1987.
Teacher	HOLY NAME BAPTIST ACADEMY	Birmingham, AL	1979 - 1988.
Teacher	HOLY CROSS SCHOOL	Birmingham, AL	1976 - 1979.

EDUCATION AND HONORS

Bachelor of Arts in American History, Mountain View College, Gadsden, AL
- Teacher of the Year, 1986, 1981

EMPLOYMENT SITUATION:

After thirty years as a policeman, John retired from the force and successfully broke into the growing industry of property management. With the real estate squeeze in the late eighties and early nineties and a low rental occupancy in the commercial buildings he managed, John was laid off after only two years. Now in his late fifties, John felt he was too old to make another job change successfully.

STRATEGIES FOR SUCCESS:

John sought a career counselor to help him overcome fears about his age and rethink his next job target. Although he wanted to explore new fields, like private security, he was attracted by the opportunities in condominium management in his area of Richmond, Virginia. He felt secure with a chronological resume stating his experience in property management. This format showed all his promotions and achievements. His self-marketing strategy was aimed at residential property management in the area, with the added advantage of his experience in security matters.

COVER LETTER STATEMENTS:

Although commercial real estate is suffering in our area, residential property management is alive and well. With my thirty-year record of police work, and two years of commercial building management, I can bring you my hands-on knowledge of property demands, and my skill in working with people and their household and safety needs.

CRITICAL VIEWPOINT:

John could have gone into security directly, but his competition would have been younger people, and his job campaign might have lasted too long to sustain his energy. By combining his most recent work in property management with his interest in security, his campaign has a better chance of succeeding much sooner.

JOHN ANGELO
279 Ralston Road
Richmond, VA 23235
(804) 555-5617

1990-1992	Century Corporate Towers	Richmond, VA

BUILDING MANAGER

Managed two 12-story twin corporate towers from early construction through completion totalling 700,000 s.f.. Directed activities for all areas:

- Operated heating, ventilation and air conditioning.
- Supervised custodial services including marble restoration.
- Coordinated corporate tenant relocation, completion of tenant suites and additional construction needs.
- Assigned maintenance personnel for building needs.
- Supervised maintenance of two six-level parking garages, corporate park roadways and all entrances.
- Managed all logistics associated with fire detection, emergency generators, security access, elevator systems, inside and outside decorative pools and general ambiance.

1960-1990	Richmond Police Department	Richmond, VA

1982-1990   LIEUTENANT

- Supervised maintenance of Richmond Police Station.
- Prepared budget requests for Support Services Division.
- Directed the installation of traffic signs, signals and road markings.
- Purchased and replaced police cruisers and oversaw the maintenance of entire fleet.
- Managed personnel in Support Services Division.
- Created computer programs for burglar alarms, accident data, and vehicle preventive maintenance systems.

1975-1982   SERGEANT

1970-1975   DETECTIVE

1960-1970   PATROL OFFICER

BOARD MEMBERSHIPS / PROFESSIONAL AFFILIATIONS:

- Richmond Civil Preparedness Advisory Board
- Police Zoning Code Enforcement Board
- Richmond Parking Authority and Community Development Committee
- Accepted as photographer in Chamber of Commerce juried show for past five years
- Building Owners' Management Association (BOMA)

EDUCATION:

1978	University of Richmond	A.S. Criminal Justice
	Graduate, FBI Academy	Quantico, VA.

EMPLOYMENT SITUATION:

Claire was a bright young organizational consultant with excellent educational and training credentials, who had had a steady string of consulting jobs since completing graduate school. She was outgoing and optimistic, but had received no job offers after ten months of what seemed to be a well-organized job campaign.

STRATEGIES FOR SUCCESS:

Claire sought counseling from a friend who helped revise her resume into a two-page combination targeted/functional format. Featuring Claire's accomplishments, as opposed to her many jobs and their sometimes unrelated functions, proved to be an important part of her career strategy.

Claire's friend was also able to analyze her interviewing patterns. He helped her to discover that her status as a consultant had unconsciously made her treat many interviewers as competitors, which probably accounted for the many frustrating months in the job market.

COVER LETTER STATEMENTS:

I understand your division has multiple organizational development needs, including that of building leadership that is both fluid and structured. Striking the right balance between participation and discipline is an age-old dilemma for managers.

I suggest that I am able to help you build exactly that kind of balance. I have been both a consultant and an employee, and so can widen my scope to consider an issue as a developmental opportunity, or narrow my sights to solving a specific problem.

CRITICAL VIEWPOINT:

Claire's counselor helped her generate more interviews with a resume that emphasized her capabilities, rather than her many "jobs." Three days after her interview counseling, Claire was offered a job at a 12 percent increase over her last salary.

(Second page covers her work history, education, and publications.)

CLAIRE BARETTA
1854 Daniels Road
Duluth, MN 55811
(218) 555-0237

OBJECTIVE: ORGANIZATIONAL DEVELOPMENT

Consulting, human relations training, team-building, and team management.

CAPABILITIES:

- Coach managers in working effectively with staff.
- Consult with groups regarding communication and group process.
- Help groups and individuals translate long-range goals into realistic strategies and appropriate action plans.
- Conduct and moderate small group discussions to develop a range of considerations about a topic, and then reach consensus.
- Assess needs and process communications to provide vivid, purposeful feedback.
- Design training programs, facilitate the process, evaluate outcomes.

ACCOMPLISHMENTS:

Consulting

- Helped district-level groups identify team-building goals and develop strategies and action plans to meet them.
- Interviewed national association executives to develop a series of reports on association management styles and development.
- Interviewed the leaders of nine community service organizations to dentify issues and concerns about interorganizational collaboration.
- Collaborated with students and faculty to formulate and develop a graduate level academic program.
- Planned and coordinated orientation and community-building programs to increase participation in departmental decision-making.

Training

- Presented seminars to managers from Fortune 500 companies on cultural differences, team building, and managing workplace diversity.
- Designed and presented self-development workshops on an entrepreneurial basis.
- Designed and delivered video-feedback programs to develop and improve job-hunters' interview techniques.
- Taught college level courses on human interaction, counseling, and interviewing skills.

Team Management

- Developed and implemented plans to facilitate production, build morale, and coordinate staff while meeting project requirements and timelines.

1992 • Cited as contributing editor in John Donohoe's book *Heading the Social Services Agencies: Balancing Staff and Volunteers.*

EMPLOYMENT SITUATION:

Malcolm sold his lawn care business after twelve years. For six months he ran a roofing business unsuccessfully and finally had to close. Although his lawn care business had succeeded, he was devastated at his failure with the roofing enterprise. Now he was tired of running his own show, and wanted to step into management for someone else.

STRATEGIES FOR SUCCESS:

From the outset Malcolm insisted on a chronological format for his resume, even though he had gaps in his work history due to military service and two unsuccessful tries at college. He had extreme difficulty verbalizing his skills and accomplishments, generally telling his career advisor, "Yes, I accomplished a few things, but that's only what you're supposed to do."

His counselor had him place his job objective at the top of the resume to focus it and create interest. Short action statements were used throughout to communicate the accomplishments. It was decided to leave out the roofing business entirely.

COVER LETTER STATEMENTS:

I am an experienced, loyal, and dedicated manager devoted to hard work and achieving high-quality results. I enjoy challenges, juggling a wide variety of details, and creating rapport with clients.

I built a highly successful lawn care business over several years. I managed all aspects of the entrepreneurial venture, including supervising workers, scheduling and managing the workload, and handling billing and payroll.

CRITICAL VIEWPOINT:

Malcolm wanted to conceal the failed roofing business, so he dropped it from his resume and interviews. It was only six months since he had sold the lawn care business; he explained to interviewers that he developed a small business that didn't take off and he wanted to close it down quickly and move on to working for others.

Malcolm's personality couldn't entertain a more creative resume approach, like the functional or targeted formats, but this was an attractive sales piece and he used it proudly.

MALCOLM BARTEL
41 Arlington Place
Portland, ME 04101
(207) 555-5807

JOB OBJECTIVE:

A management position to include skills in purchasing, supervision, basic business administration, and motivation of people.

WORK EXPERIENCE:

1978-Present   AAA Lawn Care   Portland, ME
                   OWNER/PROPRIETOR

- Created business devoted to total residential lawn care.
- Managed all aspects of the venture, including hiring, supervision, and buying.
- Initiated advertising campaigns, invoicing, accounts receivable.
- Planned work schedules of six employees.
- Dealt effectively with customers and general public.
- Created significant repeat business due to outstanding rapport.

1974-1978   City of Portland   Portland, ME
                   BUYER/EXPEDITER

- Purchased variety of items for all city departments.
- Created relations with vendors; expedited and followed up on all transactions.
- Served as Special Assistant to the Purchasing Agent.

1967-1971   United States Air Force
                   PROCUREMENT SPECIALIST

- Purchased for the United States Air Force.
- Managed contractual maintenance services and administered construction contracts from excavation through finished product.

EDUCATION: LaGrange Community College—Business Administration

                Successfully completed Procurement Specialist School, Amarillo, TX, and purchasing courses offered by the federal government.

EMPLOYMENT SITUATION:

Veronica wanted to change from a human resources generalist to the speciality of benefits administrator. Only her two most recent years' experience (out of fifteen years at work) contributed directly to her goal. Her degree in education was totally unrelated. Although the career change was within her industry, Veronica felt nervous about presenting herself as a benefits specialist.

STRATEGIES FOR SUCCESS:

Veronica's career advisor helped her choose the most relevant qualifications to support the benefits job and to emphasize these and her Employee Benefits Specialist certification rather than her longer history as a generalist.

COVER LETTER STATEMENTS:

As benefits administrator for a multi-industrial corporation for the past two years, I demonstrated broad competence in many facets of benefits administration, including:

- Self-insured welfare plans

  - Medical, dental, vision, and prescription

  - Drug plans

  - Flexible spending and dependent care accounts

  - Disability plans

- Defined benefit pension plans

- Benefit cost control

- Flexible benefit plans

I have an advanced degree and will shortly achieve my CEBS certification. My background in benefits is complemented by nine years' prior experience as a human resource generalist.

CRITICAL VIEWPOINT:

Veronica took the two years of her position in benefits, and stretched and detailed them over the entire first page of her resume. As her company was very large and well-known, her experience and accomplishments demonstrated breadth and depth.

(Second page covers two other semi-related jobs held over thirteen years, as well as education and memberships.)

VERONICA BRAUNSTEIN
7232 Old Fairburn Road
Atlanta, GA 30349
(404) 555-9235

CASWELL HARDISON, INC.   Atlanta, GA   1991–Present
Benefits Administrator

Provide benefit services and administer the following union and salaried
benefit plans for 800 active employees and 5,500 retired and vested plan
participants for Caswell Hardison Group contributing $1.3 billion to the total
annual sales of $2.4 billion:

* Retirement plans—four defined benefit plans
* Savings plan—401 K plan
* Self-insured welfare plans
    Medical, dental, vision, and prescription drug plans
    Flexible spending and dependent care programs
    Disability plans
    Flexible benefits plan for active salaried employees
* Life insurance

- Resolve problems and respond to pension and welfare plan
  inquiries up-lined by Benefits Assistants.
- Developed rapport with third party administrators for smooth
  coordination of projects and tasks.
- Coordinate Benefits department workload reducing response time
  to benefit inquiries to two weeks.
- Provide timely and accurate data to auditors and actuaries.
- Maintain mainframe Human Resource System and extract reports
  and information using GRS (General Retrieval System).
- Developed PC applications for pension and insurance
  administration using Lotus 1-2-3.
- Improved accuracy and reduced time required to calculate salaried
  pensions by revising the Lotus 1-2-3 pension calculation disk in
  accordance with formula changes and by adding macros for easier
  data entry.
- Collected, summarized, and reconciled pension valuation data
  for four defined benefits plans meeting all deadlines set by actuary.
- Involved in development and administration of newly designed
  flexible benefits plan successfully implemented January 1, 1993.
- Responsible for final review of all pension calculations and
  adjustments.
- Cut budgeted expense by 35% producing savings of $65,000 for
  Medicare Catastrophic reimbursements through analysis of
  experience and careful selection of vendor for payment processing
  and tax reporting.

Volunteer Income Tax Assistance Program

EMPLOYMENT SITUATION:

James and Nancy sought advice to help bring about their long-term goal of owning and operating a Bed-and-Breakfast. They decided to test this goal by first managing an apartment complex. Although the more intimate nature of a B-and-B would not be experienced in this first step, they could be learning how to solve similar problems in managing real estate for a multiple-family residence.

STRATEGIES FOR SUCCESS:

Both people, each with very different work histories, had to be marketed together. They decided to use a single one-page resume, with individual work histories attached. James and Nancy did extensive information interviewing with property management firms. They targeted the ones they liked best, and sent them their resume package.

They both worked diligently to translate the language of their career histories to the jargon of their targeted job. The resume had to show a complementarity between them, indicating that they were two halves of one terrific whole.

COVER LETTER STATEMENTS:

Your frank discussion of the overall challenges of your industry was helpful in allowing us to see where our strengths can counterbalance your potential problems in meeting the needs of your tenants.

We feel we have a truly winning combination of skill and personality, and would appreciate another short meeting to further discuss opportunities at your new Hanover development in West County. As Nancy is available immediately, she could meet with potential tenants during your pre-sales period.

CRITICAL VIEWPOINT:

James and Nancy's skills combine well to fit the job description. Their attached individual employment histories list their jobs, titles, and dates of employment. As James is comfortable on the phone, he handled that part of their campaign, while Nancy, who makes a great first impression, attended initial meetings.

(Second and third pages cover individual work histories.)

JAMES and NANCY BRIDGES
421 Exmoor Place, Eugene, OR 97404
(503) 555-5732

OBJECTIVE:
To use our managing, organizing and communicating abilities in a property management organization.

MANAGEMENT/ADMINISTRATION:
Nancy manages a high-volume restaurant, supervising 70 employees, to insure quality customer service.
- Directs hiring, interviewing and training, resulting in low turnover and minimal training costs.
- Develops strong customer and employee relations and promotes satisfaction.
- Motivates employees through positive reinforcement, achieving high productivity.
- Problem-solves with employees and customers, developing overall harmony.

James manages an orthopedic, neurosurgeon and general medicine out-patient clinic.
- Schedules appointments for 750 patients per month.
- Performs daily office management duties, resulting in good patient/staff relations.
- Problem-solves for patients, directing priority cases to doctors.
- Has broad skills in communicating by phone or in person.

DEALING WITH PEOPLE:
Nancy has had many years of experience dealing with the public.
- Waiting on tables and bartending involved a wide variety of people skills, while developing rapport.
- Freelanced working in media promotions, and catered private parties.
- Volunteered for the YWCA hospitality team.

James has a wide variety of people skills.
- Promoted a bicycle touring company by directing tours and developing customer rapport.
- Dealt with public relations, employee and customer satisfaction, while managing a service-oriented business.

MONEY MANAGEMENT:
Nancy conducted inventory and cost controls within budget, decreasing overhead costs.
- Is completely trained in daily bookkeeping, preparation of operating statements and profit-and-loss statements.
- Assembled and produced payroll.
- Has a working knowledge of preparing sales projections.

MAINTENANCE:
James has practical experience in home maintenance.
- Fixing leaking faucets, broken toilets, clogged drains.
- Designed and built a workshop, installed window molding, re-roofed homes and built patios.
- Rewiring electrical fixtures.

Nancy has working knowledge of quality home maintenance.
- Painting, wallpapering, hardwood floor care and cleaning procedures.

EMPLOYMENT SITUATION:

Jocelyn took early retirement from the telephone company after thirty years of service. Since her husband had recently passed away, she wanted to create a new career by becoming a concierge in a hotel. This was a long-held dream for her, a career for which she felt capable, in an environment that would stimulate her natural affability and sociability and would keep her mentally active.

Jocelyn had no background in this field, although she did have some related experience. The challenge was to make the transition believable.

STRATEGIES FOR SUCCESS:

Jocelyn's counselor suggested a functional format with the job target at the top of the resume. They decided also to emphasize her strong work ethic and relationship to service, translating her skills from telephone industry jargon into language compatible with this new line of work. They used titles that were related to the job objective, such as "hospitality."

COVER LETTER STATEMENTS:

Over the years, I have developed the expertise, personality, and personal appearance that would serve you and your guests well in reception or hospitality positions. As a professional with the Bell System, I developed mastery in dealing with the public, and I have adapted easily to new environments. I have trained many individuals, and drawn upon diverse skills in various positions, directing numerous special projects within my company.

CRITICAL VIEWPOINT:

Note that there is no apology or hesitation in Jocelyn's approach. The self-marketing statements affirm her study and understanding of what a hotel concierge must be and do. The resume highlights customer-oriented skills that she had in fact developed over the years. She left out her job titles, which her counselor felt would be unnecessary with such a dramatic career change.

JOCELYN CARMICHAEL
8442 Appleton Drive
St. Louis, MO 63132
(314) 555-2100 Messages

OBJECTIVE: CONCIERGE—HOTEL INDUSTRY

COMMUNICATIONS / HOSPITALITY:

- Handled variety of clerical/social functions including reception, entertaining, and making people of diverse interests and economic status feel comfortable.
- Coordinated and oversaw two Ameritech Regional conferences that were highly acclaimed (attended by 2000 and 6000 each).
- Accustomed to accepting responsibility, delegating authority and working with people of all ages.
- Wrote surveys to determine customer ideas; developed correspondence that enhanced customer support and calculated impact of various programs.
- Coordinated many community events including Pace Setter activities.
- Participated in wide variety of diverse activities including United Negro College Scholarship Fund, WBI Person-to-Person Friendly Visit Program, and the Juneau Village Ronald McDonald Charity.

MANAGEMENT:

- Supervised 10 to 15 associates and effectively helped develop careers.
- Assisted in the creation of consumer market education recommendations and new employee orientation programs.
- Initiated and coordinated human resource programs for a broad variety of populations. Acknowledged for outstanding dedication and follow-up.
- Developed projects with attention to detail and timely, cost-effective, high-quality results.

WORK EXPERIENCE:

1962–1992 SOUTHWESTERN BELL TELEPHONE
Various positions, including middle management

1975–Present
Volunteer—Welcome Wagon, March of Dimes, American Cancer Society and others previously listed

EDUCATION:

Successfully completed numerous management and personal development courses.
High School Graduate/Scholarship to Nursing School

EMPLOYMENT SITUATION:

Joseph rose to the top of his company to become second-in-command. Eight years ago he purchased a small interest in the company but knew all along he wanted to run his own show. He convinced the president to buy him out, and sought career counseling to organize his next move.

STRATEGIES FOR SUCCESS:

Joseph wanted to appeal to financial institutions to back his new construction business. To protect himself, however, he and his counselor prepared two resumes, one for another corporate management position, and one to apply for financing. The latter example is included here.

COVER LETTER STATEMENTS:

My business financial record has been impeccable over the past twenty years, and so I know I am able to carry the same level of responsibility as I establish my own construction business.

My business plan is fully developed, and there are several people interested in investing, so I'm ready and anxious to move forward quickly.

CRITICAL VIEWPOINT:

Joseph had been an entrepreneur operating within someone else's business for years. His relationship with his career counselor was useful to help him organize and package himself appropriately to get his business going quickly. It worked. He obtained both financing and a dynamic partner, and now has more business than he can accept.

JOSEPH G. CARROLL
612 North River Road
Fargo, ND 58102
Office: (701) 555-2582
Residence: (701) 555-1929

SUMMARY:

Over 22 years experience of commercial and industrial construction including general management, planning, finance, and accounting.

WORK HISTORY:

1991-Present	**PLAINS CONSTRUCTION, President**	Fargo, ND
1970-1991	**SOUTER CONSTRUCTION COMPANY**	Fargo, ND
1980-1991	**Executive Vice President, Secretary/Treasurer**	
1975-1980	**Treasurer, Assistant Treasurer**	
1970-1975	**Accounting Supervisor, Accountant**	

ACCOMPLISHMENTS:

- Joined Souter in 1970 when it was doing $6 million in volume. Purchased a share in the business in 1984 when the volume was $16 million and grew it to $36 million in 1991.

- Developed a reputation as one of the premier Fargo contracting companies known for its high quality, reasonable cost projects.

- Contracts ranged from small renovations to a $20-million plus project.

- Scope of services included construction management, designing-building, and negotiating and bidding general construction.

- Had primary responsibility for the company's financial affairs, dealing with three financial institutions. Negotiated seven-figure bank lines of credit and mortgages. Banking relations were such that security requirements were not increased during periods of losses.

- Purchased and managed all corporate insurance and surety bonds. Achieved one of the lowest ratings in the Fargo area for a construction company on Workers Compensation, business auto, general and excess liability. Reduced insurance costs by approximately 30% by implementing a safety program.

- Designed and implemented a highly sophisticated financial information system that included detailed project accounting.

- Had key responsibility for establishing the direction of the company and providing daily management.

EDUCATION:

B.S.B.A. (Accounting), Notre Dame University, South Bend, IN, 1968.

EMPLOYMENT SITUATION:

Terry was an Administrative Director when her firm asked her to lay off 20 percent of her staff due to a business downturn. At this point, she paused to take stock of her own work situation. She was overworked and exhausted. Her recent divorce had spurred her to realize it was time for a change, time to elevate her sights after she'd been "plateaued" for several years.

Terry was afraid of the next step but longed for new adventures. She had many friends in Cleveland, where she lived, but was willing to move if she found a great job elsewhere.

STRATEGIES FOR SUCCESS:

Terry rolled out her campaign city-by-city in Cleveland, Columbus, Chicago, St. Louis, and Indianapolis. Her goal was to go after professional service jobs in accounting, law, and consulting. A chronological resume suited her objective perfectly.

COVER LETTER STATEMENTS:

As an experienced Administrative Director, I have spent sixteen years initiating, building, restructuring, and improving the productivity of two professional services firms. This is work I find challenging and rewarding, and I have made a substantial difference in how smoothly these professional teams operate.

Now I am seeking to relocate and apply my skills to an expanding firm like yours. My resume is enclosed for your review.

CRITICAL VIEWPOINT:

Terry also answered ads, worked her professional networks, and stayed a week in Chicago at a friend's while interviewing at as many firms as she could. She loved the city, and ended up in a very large law firm as Manager of Administration, reporting to an Executive Partner and earning a much better compensation package than she had previously earned.

(Second page covers thirteen years with a previous employer, her education, and her professional affiliations and community activities.)

THERESA CORSA
3356 Cachepit Way
Cleveland, OH 44227
(216) 555-3413 office
(216) 555-8026 home

OBJECTIVE:

Senior Administrator to direct the staffing, policy administration, benefits, and office operations of a professional service organization.

SUMMARY:

Experienced architectural and engineering firm Director of Administration with 16 years hands-on management of multimillion-dollar budgets, staffs of up to 75, and administrative support services, including computerized systems and procedures.

EXPERIENCE:

1990–Present   JAVIER, GOULD & HENNINGS—ARCHITECTS

DIRECTOR OF ADMINISTRATION—Cleveland

Initiated, built, and directed administrative operations for the firm's five domestic and two European offices. Operations included administrative and secretarial support, word processing, maintenance, purchasing/supplies, duplication, records, telephone, travel reservations, mail/messenger, and cafeteria units. Managed staff of 75 and a budget of four million dollars.

- Restructured the administrative organization and recruited strong personnel to head the Management Information Systems function during a period of rapid growth for the firm.
- Implemented a stratified monthly financial reporting structure to distribute more sophisticated operations expense data to senior management.
- Initiated conversion of minicomputer/stand-alone PC-based word processing system to a local area network configuration.
- Converted AT&T "Dimension 2000" telephone system to a state-of-the-art "System 85."
- Negotiated revised health and life insurance benefits for the firm's 125 partners and employees.
- Attended all Executive Committee meetings and participated in decisions relating to administrative procedures and nonarchitectural staff matters.

Association of Professional Administrators

EMPLOYMENT SITUATION:

Neil, most recently a pharmacy manager, wanted a radical career change. He was leaving the field of health care after seventeen years to switch to small business management, preferably in a service company. Fundamentally introverted, Neil was not given to selling himself. However, with a recently completed M.B.A., he was eager to identify a number of small businesses and move on to a new line of work. He did not want to overly focus his resume, wishing to spread his net for potential business far and wide.

STRATEGIES FOR SUCCESS:

First, his counselor helped Neil generalize his entire work history. All of the medical/pharmaceutical jargon had to be translated into words that any small business owner could understand. The counselor also helped him to see that his greatest strengths were his analytical and detail/organizational abilities. As an introvert unable to change his basic nature, he knew he didn't want to manage people, just operations.

COVER LETTER STATEMENTS:

My enclosed resume reflects my interest in a change. I have spent seventeen successful years in the field of health care, honing my skills in operations management. Now my focus is in other areas of business. I have recently completed an M.B.A., and am eager to combine my project management skills with my knowledge of strategic planning.

My knowledge of your company convinces me that I would be a good addition to the management of your Minnesota chain of dry goods stores.

CRITICAL VIEWPOINT:

Neil did a really good job of eliminating the medical/pharmaceutical language from his resume. If one reads the resume carefully, the language emphasizes operations skills and minimizes people skills. This is a well-considered strategy for making a dramatic transition.

Neil Crabtree
5248 Colonial Drive
Minneapolis, MN 55416
Home: (612) 555- 6462

OBJECTIVE: Business operations manager to conduct planning, communicate alternatives and assist in implementation. The results should be reduced costs, increased sales and improved operations.

QUALIFICATIONS

- Excellent analytical skills
- Goal-oriented
- Well-organized
- Very effective communicator
- Consistent record of growth and responsibility

ACHIEVEMENTS

- Developed and instituted an inventory control system that increased stock turnover and decreased inventory value by 50% for a savings of $150,000.
- Maintained daily purchasing, shipping/receiving operations of a $10 million/year branch.
- Improved inventory control by designing systems and initiating their use to monitor product use, expense and variance.
- Wrote and published two textbook chapters and a journal article.
- Implemented and supervised a series of programs of sterile product preparation.

EXPERIENCE

1990–1992	Healthwell. **Operations Manager.** Directed daily business operations. Responsibilities included computer operations, purchasing, inventory control, accounts payable, quality assurance, hiring/firing, leases, traffic control.
1987–1990	Minneapolis General Hospital. **Manager of Support Services.** Facilitated purchasing and inventory control. Initiated and maintained a system for analysis of department statistics.
1981–1987	Harwick Hospital. **Supervisor.** Prepared and monitored $10 million budget. Supervised sterile product preparation and a staff of 45.
1975–1981	Graham Hospital. **Staff Pharmacist.** Trained and supervised 13 technicians.

EDUCATION

- M. B. A., University of Minneapolis (concentration in finance)
- B. S., University of Wisconsin

AFFILIATED ACTIVITIES

- American Management Association
- Minnesota Hospital Association, Advisory Committee. Awarded vendor contracts for a four-state area.
- Streamside Homeowners Association, President and Vice-President
- Lectured university students.

EMPLOYMENT SITUATION:

Adrienne worked for one company for eleven years before following her spouse on a relocation from Houston to Detroit. Her company would gladly have transferred her, but they had no Detroit division. She loved her work and wanted to stay in quality management/organizational development. Neither Adrienne nor her husband had a Detroit network to tap.

STRATEGIES FOR SUCCESS:

With her counselor, Adrienne worked out a good chronological "generalist" resume, focusing on strengths that seemed applicable to the auto industry. She also required some coaching in interview techniques to facilitate the translation of her skills across industries. She learned that her professional credentials would be appealing to any large industry.

COVER LETTER STATEMENTS:

Your division is one to which I would like to contribute as I make a move to the Detroit area. I have over ten years' experience as an Industrial Engineer for Westfield Chemical Company.

For the last six years, my focus was quality management/systems analysis, resulting in improvement of productivity and performance in manufacturing facilities. From my enclosed resume, you will see that I have both leadership and team-playing skills. I would like very much to continue my commitment to quality management with your company.

I plan to be in the Detroit area from July 1–10, and will call you on June 28 to make an appointment. If you wish to reach me sooner, please call.

CRITICAL VIEWPOINT:

Adrienne has a lot going for her. She's current in a field that is growing. She's seeking to move from one Fortune 500 company to another, a company that is also known to actively use quality management, team-building methods. By describing herself at the top of her resume as a consultant, she leaves the door open for either an internal placement or an external consulting position.

Adrienne Cusack
92 Purple Sage Road
Houston, TX 77049
Residence: (713) 555-3614
Office: (713) 555-2290

OBJECTIVE: Quality Management/improvement Consultant

QUALIFICATIONS:
- Over ten years experience with a major corporation
- Skills in assessing and evaluating customer requirements and business objectives
- Developing and deploying organization-wide improvement strategies
- Integrating organizational designs with interlocking natural unit teams
- Matching skill-development needs with appropriate level and delivery of training
- Designing systems and internal support for continual improvement
- Implementing and follow-up consulting to put principles into practice

EXPERIENCE:

1983–Present	Westfield Chemical Company (WCC), Houston, Texas
1990–1992	Westfield Photo Division Company (WPD), Atlanta, Georgia
1992–Present	**Quality Management Consultant:** Consultant for both WCC's Administrative Organization Redesign process and strategic intent initiative. Maintained full responsibility for developing and implementing plans/courses of action for several management and technical teams.
1990–1992	**Westfield Photo Quality Core Team:** Original member responsible for initiating and leading the WP Quality Leadership Process in two of the largest business units, three major support organizations and the Latin American region impacting close to 3000 employees. In addition, developed an infrastructure of internal consultants through training and consultation.
1988–1990	**Pilot of Team Management** in Textile Fibers Division: Coordinator for entire Team Management effort with full responsibility for seventy interlocking teams. As a design team member, pioneered planning, implementing, and coaching facets of the quality process.
1983–1988	**Project Industrial Engineer and Systems Analyst** for two manufacturing divisions.

EDUCATION: B. S. in Industrial Engineering/Operations Research, Texas A & M University, 1983

SUPPORTING DATA: Formal Quality Training, Swarthbone Institute: Quality Management/Leadership Process; Team Management Consultant Training; Performance Management; Decision-Making Styles; Listening skills; Deming philosophy; Statistical Methods; Problem Solving and Group Dynamics.

PROFESSIONAL AFFILIATIONS: Institute of Industrial Engineers; have served in all officer capacities. American Society of Quality Control; maintain active role in local chapter.

EMPLOYMENT SITUATION:

Geraldine was a teacher who had stayed home to raise her children for thirteen years. Like many other mothers she had been active in a lot of volunteer work. Despite her many skills as a volunteer, Geraldine nevertheless doubted her employability.

Geraldine was not able to relocate and wanted to teach in a suburban school district. She needed to integrate in her presentation both her paid teaching and her unpaid volunteer experience.

STRATEGIES FOR SUCCESS:

For Geraldine's campaign, her counselor suggested a full-fledged business strategy—cold-calling to principals. Geraldine understood that she would get nowhere just mailing a resume and then sitting around waiting to hear from people. She was assertive in spite of her self-doubts, and put herself way ahead of the competition. With this very businesslike and positive approach, she generated a high number of interviews.

COVER LETTER STATEMENTS:

As a licensed professional teacher with experience in private and public education, I have skills in classroom teaching of the entire range of primary-level subjects. As a Sunday school superintendent and coordinator for Vacation Bible School, I can also offer administrative skills.

In my recent experience as a substitute teacher, I have noticed that the curriculum is not fully absorbed, and that the special-needs children on both ends of the spectrum are barely holding on. These are children who usually do not obtain special education status, but who do need individual attention. As a reading tutor (volunteer), I have developed techniques that can unify the uneven learning patterns in a large classroom. I'd like to meet with you and demonstrate how these work.

CRITICAL VIEWPOINT:

Geraldine is definitely a risk-taker in the educational field. In her volunteer work, without the pressure of supervision, she made innovative discoveries that she feels would deeply enhance her contributions to the classroom.

Her resume is chronological. This format is possible because her volunteer church experience is so rich and diversified that it easily compensates for gaps in her professional teaching experience.

GERALDINE DOWNES
12250 Castleberry Place
Affton, MO 63123
(314) 555-9864

HOLY REDEEMER LUTHERAN CHURCH   Affton, MO
Church began as a mission congregation and has grown to over 350 members.

Pastoral Assistant, Confirmation Teacher/Superintendent   1985–Present
Served in all administrative and specific education functions. Activities included office
administration, coordination duties, secretarial support and church council.
Accomplishments include:

- Serving as Sunday School Superintendent. Oversee all education and
  supervisory needs of a very successful program that includes over 100
  primary-grade children.
- Served as chairperson after developing the Christian Education Committee
  that is responsible for all Christian education from three-year-olds to adults.
- Regularly taught Sunday School and Confirmation classes ranging in size
  from 10 to 20 students.
- Developed and directed Vacation Bible School. Specifically worked with a
  team of six teachers to write and choose curriculum. Coordinated student
  registration, ordered materials and collected fees.

PUBLIC EDUCATION EXPERIENCE   1974–Present

Substitute Teacher   1992–Present
Third and Fourth Grades   1977–1981
Teacher's Aide   1976–1977
Third and Fourth Grades   1974–1975

FORMAL EDUCATION

B.S.—Elementary Education—high honors—University of Missouri.
Admitted to Phi Beta Kappa Society.
Studied abroad at Redland College, Bristol, England.
Continued graduate work at the University of Missouri.
Studied"On the Write Road" and "Discipline with Love and Logic" through the
Webster University Continuing Education Program.

**PROFESSIONAL CERTIFICATIONS, SERVICE PERSONAL
AND ACTIVITIES**

Missouri teacher certification (1-8), Illinois teacher certification (K-6).
Actively involved in community services including individual reading
tutor program for children.
Volunteer in elementary classrooms, Brownie leader, and newsletter author.

EMPLOYMENT SITUATION:

Lawrence had had a steady thirteen-year career in personnel with a major computer corporation when he was recruited by a smaller company. After three years, this company "downsized" and a 15 percent staff cut eliminated his job. Lawrence was determined to advance his career opportunities and at least maintain his current salary.

STRATEGIES FOR SUCCESS:

Lawrence targeted manufacturing industries although he was concerned about his lack of recent experience in manufacturing. His counselor helped him to update an already outstanding chronological resume. Lawrence tapped his extensive personal network and obtained the names of numerous CEO's in manufacturing. His campaign was to mine the hidden job market, answer ads, and utilize headhunters who already knew his reputation.

COVER LETTER STATEMENTS:

[This was sent to the CEO of a large manufacturing firm.]

I know that your office has received hundreds of responses to the advertisement for Human Resources Director. I want to do everything I can to insure that my qualifications will be thoroughly evaluated, so I am taking the liberty of sending a copy of my resume to you directly.

I hold a master's degree in Industrial Relations and have more than fifteen years of comprehensive human resource management experience in a variety of business environments. I'd like to meet with you personally to discuss my ability to interface effectively with all organizational levels in the development and implementation of human resource strategies, which will improve the productivity and effectiveness of your company.

CRITICAL VIEWPOINT:

Lawrence's accomplishments were excellent. However, although he had had direct involvement in manufacturing during his early years at Compu-Master, that wasn't enough to justify a functional resume.

(Second page covers early history, education, and articles/publications.)

LAWRENCE K. EMMANS
582 King Creek Road
Minneapolis, MN 55416
Office: (612) 555-8058
Home: (612) 555-7586

UNIVERSAL APPRAISAL ASSOCIATES—Minneapolis, MN
Universal Appraisal is the world's largest appraisal and valuation consulting firm.

Director of Human Resources   1989–Present
Responsible for all corporate human resource functions including compensation
and benefits, training and development and special employee relations programs for
this 800-employee, $70 million firm.
- Produced significant savings in employment and benefits costs while
  improving effectiveness in both areas.
- Professionalized the human resource function without an increase in the budget.
- Installed dual-career, succession planning and professional development
  programs for managers and technical staff.
- Improved accountability throughout the firm through an improved system of
  performance management.

COMPU-MASTER CORPORATION—Chicago, Il   1976–1989
Compu-Master is a $3.6B computer systems and services company engaged in
developing, manufacturing, marketing and supporting information systems.

Director of Personnel and Administration   1988–1989
Responsible for all human resource support and training for Business Advisors
Consulting Service, a $30 million business unit.
- Produced specialized compensation programs and installed systems for
  executive development.
- Managed the restructuring and downsizing of the work force in a rapidly
  evolving business environment.

Director of Employee Relations   1985–1988
Directed a highly specialized employee relations department which provided
ombudsman services and identified, diagnosed, and resolved employee work-related
problems. Also provided quality assurance for the company's grievance system.
- Developed a staff of specialized counselors.
- Installed a nationally recognized peer review grievance system featured in the
  Harvard Business Review.
- Successfully expanded employee problem-assistance program to international
  affiliates.

Unpublished manuscript

EMPLOYMENT SITUATION:

Floyd was over fifty and had run his own paint contracting business for the past ten years. He was financially successful but personally burned out. He had a past work history of book buying, as well as long and successful experience as a volunteer in diverse areas of public service in Allentown, and now wanted a new career in nonprofit administration.

STRATEGIES FOR SUCCESS:

When Floyd came to counseling, he was clear about what he wanted but not confident he could sell himself, even with all his volunteer experience. The strategy was first to provide him with a professional credit in nonprofit work, so he enrolled at a local college and obtained a Certificate of Nonprofit Administration. He also joined two nonprofit associations, rising to head one of them in just over six months. By the time he put his resume together, 75 percent of it represented experience in nonprofit organizations. He used his volunteer network to set himself up with high-level information interviews.

COVER LETTER STATEMENTS:

I am ready to use all my years of volunteer experience in administering a growing nonprofit organization with your track record for excellence. My ten years of experience as an independent business owner would help immensely in organizing your currently overburdened case load. I am willing and able to take over a mountain of administrative detail and transform it into a smoothly running operating arm of your agency.

CRITICAL VIEWPOINT:

Floyd and his counselor prepared a strong presentation, translating the language of the paint contracting business and bookstore management into administrative accomplishments. Note that the nonprofit history is separated from and placed before the work history.

The Highlights of Qualifications section is well written and really sells Floyd's history and current career goal.

FLOYD L. ERDOS
151 Marantha Way
Allentown, PA 18106
(215) 555-6212

OBJECTIVE: ADMINISTRATOR IN A NONPROFIT ORGANIZATION

HIGHLIGHTS OF QUALIFICATIONS

- Over twenty-five years of management and administrative experience.
- Vice-president and committee chair for three nonprofit organizations.
- Certification in nonprofit administration.

PROFESSIONAL EXPERIENCE

ADMINISTRATION AND MANAGEMENT

- Coordinated and delegated over two hundred volunteers for three nonprofit organizations.
- Managed three bookstores, purchased stock, trained and supervised twelve employees; responsible for $400,000 volume.
- Managed and operated successful paint contracting business, prepared cost projections, payroll and business reports.
- Supervised, trained, and evaluated ten employees, maintained inventory and production quotas for catalog division of retail store.

COMMUNICATION

- Made group presentations to gain approval and funding for three nonprofit organizations.
- Wrote grant proposal, evaluated direct mail campaign, wrote news releases for the Allentown Public Library.
- Compiled and edited production, budget, and customer satisfaction reports for catalog division of retail store.
- Served as liaison between bookstore staff, faculty, and college directors.

NONPROFIT HISTORY

Internship	Allentown Public Library	1993
Vice-President, Committee Chairman	St. Mark's Lutheran Church	1992, 1990
Park Host	Allegheny County Open Space	1992
Committee Chairman	Boy Scouts	1991
Speakers Bureau Volunteer	Alleco Action-Center	1989

WORK HISTORY

Bookbuyer	Moffett College Books	1986–present
Painting Contractor	Self-Employed	1982–1992
Bookstore Manager, Assistant Manager	Chapter 6 and Muhlenberg College	1978–1982

EDUCATION/PROFESSIONAL DEVELOPMENT

Certificate, Nonprofit Administration, Muhlenberg College   1993
B.A. Penn State University
Member—Pennsylvania Association of Non-Profit Organizations (PENPO)
Director of Volunteers in Agencies (DOVIA)

EMPLOYMENT SITUATION:

Max had been retired for three years from a corporate executive career when he became restless. He formed a small consulting group with his wife and three other retired executives (all in their mid-fifties). Their focus was on helping private-sector, not-for-profit organizations in their business administration systems, marketing strategies and programs, and fund-raising.

STRATEGIES FOR SUCCESS:

Max sought advice regarding presentation and pricing of his skills and services. A consulting specialist suggested he write a biography to set him apart from the competition. His marketing strategy was to reach the person at the top, either the Board Chairman, CEO, or Executive Director. He did not enclose his biography when cold-writing to leads, but every letter he wrote was highly specific to that individual. He offered his biography only after an interview with positive potential.

COVER LETTER STATEMENTS:

In three years my firm doubled contributions to the United Fund in a city similar to yours. Our capabilities in organizing systems and media strategies, and in inspiring volunteers, have been successful in dozens of other fundraising efforts. For example, we accomplished the following:

- designed a museum support campaign that increased annual giving from $20,000 to $75,000, and raised $1 million for a new building;

- developed a new community center in a suburb of a major city, raising $2.5 million for the building, and established an effective management team;

- won a Fortune Magazine award for our design of a direct mail campaign for a college's annual giving program.

Our fees are performance-based against advances. I would be pleased to discuss details of how the Ewing Group could be of service to you.

CRITICAL VIEWPOINT:

Max set himself and his group apart in charging by results, not by project. His self-marketing letter was his primary written sales piece. His biography served to fill in his background and capabilities. This approach appeals to many consulting retirees who want a low-key but effective presentation.

Biography ....

Maxwell Ewing
37 Howell St
Ossining, NY 10484
(914) 555-2031

Ewing Group
Business Consultants

Based on fifteen years of account executive experience in both advertising and public relations, Max Ewing now heads a group of five similarly experienced professionals. During his tenure with main-line firms, he designed and implemented dozens of programs both for not-for-profit and for-profit private sector institutions. These programs included speeches for CEO's and senior executives, magazine and newspaper articles and publicity, direct mail audio-visual campaigns.

With the Ewing Group, he has specialized in the business administration and business development fields for not-for-profit organizations such as schools, museums, libraries and hospitals. Annual Giving campaigns have had one-year increases ranging from 40 to 100 percent. Successful capital campaigns have ranged from $100,000 to as much as $2.5 million for a new community center in a New York City suburb. He has completed numerous strategy and feasibility studies concerning reorganization and controls systems, training in constituency relationships, and media relationships.

Mr. Ewing has an undergraduate degree from Cornell University in Psychology and English, and an M.B.A. in Communications from the Wharton School. He served for five years as a Communications Officer in the U.S. Navy, and for five years as the Chief Development Officer for a Midwestern liberal arts college.

Mr. Ewing resides in Ossining, New York with his wife, who is also a member of the Ewing Group. He is an accomplished violinist, and is active in local church and community affairs.

EMPLOYMENT SITUATION:

Walter was a powerful senior executive who had been recruited from a good job by a company offering great promise for his future. Caught in a complex management change, he was overlooked for a promotion. Now forty-seven and at the peak of his abilities, he decided to get his credentials on paper, call in his large network of contacts, and move on.

STRATEGIES FOR SUCCESS:

Walter gave sixty days' notice and asked to be allowed to conduct his job campaign half-time from his office, on full pay. The Executive Council agreed and fully supported his personal outplacement strategy. His on-the-job performance, even while working half-time, was as good as ever; his calendar of new job interviews was consistently full.

He used a chronological two-page resume highlighting his outstanding achievements.

COVER LETTER STATEMENTS:

I am an accomplished senior executive, currently responsible for marketing, distributing, and strategic planning. My background is mainly in managing food/nonfood-packaging marketing activities for a Fortune 500 division. I have a record of promotions for consistent excellence in meeting sales, profitability, and market development objectives.

My specific strengths include designing new product development programs, providing direction to the R&D functions in developing major new product programs, formulating pricing and product-line rationalization strategies that result in dramatic improvements in profitability, and devising more cost-effective distribution methods.

CRITICAL VIEWPOINT:

Walter used his career counselor to keep himself buoyant and free from depression and anger. He also put together resumes, cover letters, and interviewing strategies, as well as an outplacement plan. Since Walter bore no grudges, he could use the company's good will to support his job campaign. An executive placement counselor steered him to a job where he obtained a 30 percent salary/compensation increase.

(Second page covers early work history, education, and military background.)

J. WALTER FERGUSON
91 Phillips Place
Stamford, CT 06906
(203) 555-0830 (O)
(203) 555-4262 (H)

1988–present   **KANE MARGATE CORPORATION** Stamford, CT.
Vice President—Marketing, HALL'S FOOD SERVICE

Have full P&L responsibility for $250 million in food-service
disposable paper and plastic product sales, i.e., budgeting, pricing,
sales and income, new product development, market research,
capital spending, production planning, advertising and promotional
programs. Provide direction to Manufacturing, Engineering, Sales,
and R&D departments in implementing product programs.

Additionally, devise and implement distribution strategies for the
company's consumer and food service product line (annual sales:
$380 million) encompassing 6000 SKU's. Lastly, manage the business
acquisition function.

Key Accomplishments

- Directed R&D and other functions in developing major new
  product line introductions.
- Through a combination of pricing, new product introductions, and
  aggressive cost control programs, managed growth of food service
  sales and income to achieve a tripling in profitability over the 1988
  to 1990 period.
- Reorganized the product service department, achieving a
  significant improvement in customer responsiveness.
- Was a key contributor to the formulation of the corporate food
  service strategy currently being implemented.

1974 - 1988   **CONSOLIDATED ALUMINUM COMPANY** Greenwich, CT.
1987 - 1988   **Director of Marketing and Business Programs**
Folding Carton Business, Paper Sector.

Responsible for $250 million in sales of packaging products; supervised
five marketing managers, a pricing group, and a business program
function—the latter responsible for developing and implementing
productivity improvements.

Key Accomplishments

- Directed business activities that led to successful introduction of
  several new products.
- Designed pricing strategies that were directly responsible for a $1+M
  improvement in profitability over the 1984–1985 period.

Accounting, Technical School of Accountancy, Houston, TX

EMPLOYMENT SITUATION:

Maude had only volunteer work experience and was now seeking to gain full-time paid employment. She had married her college sweetheart, a ministry student, and joined him in earning a master's degree in divinity. They had no children, so Maude worked in the ministry without pay, first in North Carolina and then in St. Louis. Her needs changed dramatically when her husband died unexpectedly, leaving her little savings and minimal insurance.

STRATEGIES FOR SUCCESS:

Maude called on lots of counseling help from her church to ease her through the grief of losing her husband. She also called on an old friend, a professional career advisor, to help market her experience and accumulated skills. They put together a one-page functional resume.

There were several local programs developing in the town in which Maude could be powerful, helping to place borderline homeless people in subsidized low-income housing. She aimed her campaign primarily in this direction, contacting all the social services agencies which interface with that specific clientele.

COVER LETTER STATEMENTS:

My social service background, combined with my divinity degree, gives me a unique hands-on view of the clientele you service in this community. Making the transition to low-income housing can be both joyous and painful for people like your clients; I can help them in their communication with their new suburban neighbors so that they can blend in and enjoy the community without fear.

CRITICAL VIEWPOINT:

All of Maude's work history was true and credible and showed tangible results for the jobs assigned. This resume reads no differently than if her work had been for pay. Maude had only to see her activities as valuable and worthy of pay in order to conduct a confident, high-energy job campaign.

MAUDE FISCHER
7213 Rhodes Avenue
St. Louis, MO 63109
(314) 555-7524

ACCOMPLISHMENTS:

ORGANIZATION

Initiated a supervised education placement in court advocacy; organized recruitment and training of volunteers; coordinated liaison between court officials, social agency and media. Chaired a student committee on social concerns and arranged special lecture series. Programmed and evaluated a video-taped panel discussion for student leaders and university administrators.

COMMUNICATION

Presented to city officials a statement urging approval of overnight shelter facility. Described court experience of assault victims in local TV appearance; wrote newsletter article on function of court volunteers. Designed and directed worship services for hospital patients. Assisted in preparing articles series on graduate student living.

COUNSELING

Provided staff support for director of family shelter. Assisted hospital personnel in dealing with illness and death. Aided abuse victims in sharing their experience. Guided homeless families toward personal and community resources. Related to students' concerns for healthy lifestyle and meaningful vocation.

EXPERIENCE:

Administrative Assistant, Overnight Shelter	St. Louis, MO	1990
Research Interviewer, Project on Homelessness	St. Louis, MO	1988
Program Assistant, Education Department	St. Louis, MO	1988
American Red Cross		
Assistant Director, Family Shelter	Fayetteville, NC	1987-88
Chaplain Intern, Kain Medical Center	Fayetteville, NC	1987
Liaison Coordinator, Court Advocacy	Fayetteville, NC	1986–87

EDUCATION:

M.Div. Theology/Philosophy, Union Theological Seminary, St. Louis, MO
B.S., Botany/Art History, University of North Carolina, Fayetteville
Specialized training in the development of programs educating clergy on topic of family violence, Atlanta, GA

EMPLOYMENT SITUATION:

A recent graduate of a prestigious school of international relations, Curtis had experience only in military work. He targeted a position in political consulting or policy-making. He was a young man entering a field of "old boys," and the first draft of his resume was excessively filled with military jargon.

STRATEGIES FOR SUCCESS:

With his career advisor, Curtis developed a functional resume highlighting skills desired for political consulting. With his counselor's guidance he translated military experience into management, research, and analysis functions. He featured his travels under the heading of "International Experience" to indicate sophistication and worldliness, and to compensate for his relative youth. Curtis also toned down the military jargon and any potentially controversial terms, like "sniper training."

COVER LETTER STATEMENTS:

I have just completed a two-year Master of Arts in International Relations at Harvard. My research and writing has included a critical study of news reporting in Vietnam, and an analysis of U.S. strategic reinforcement of NATO. I've studied economic policy issues intensively. My exploration of the history and current status of the Third World and the Middle East have further broadened my international perspective.

Prior to coming to Harvard, I served for three years as an infantry officer in the Marine Corps, where I developed strong leadership and management skills. Responsible for Marine training as well as for personnel development, I conceived, planned, and executed operations and programs involving up to 200 men. I feel this combination of operational experience, knowledge of history and international affairs, and leadership skills will enable me to succeed in a variety of professional environments.

CRITICAL VIEWPOINT:

Curtis is still exploring the market in his covering letter by setting up exploratory interviews. He makes many strong points, but doesn't actually hard-sell. His excellent education and Marine credentials are at the top of his resume, as his experience is still that of a young man without an "old boy" track record.

CURTIS FITCH II
84 Lavalier Avenue #14
Cambridge, MA 02138
(617) 555-1507

EDUCATION
The Harvard School of Law and Diplomacy, Harvard University, Cambridge, MA.
Master of Arts in International Relations, May 1993.

Ames College, Dover, DE. B.A. May 1988. 3.7 GPA in major.
Nominated for Harry S. Truman National Scholarship.

PROFESSIONAL EXPERIENCE
Research Assistant, Harvard Law School, 1992–1993.
Liaison Officer, 1st Battalion, 1st Marines, Camp Pendleton, CA., 1991–1992.
Surveillance and Target Acquisition Platoon Commander, 1991.
Executive Officer/Platoon Commander, Bravo Company, 1989–1991.

SKILLS SUMMARY
Leadership / Training / Program Development
• Chief Instructor for Squad Leader courses; developed a comprehensive program of instruction and field training to teach leadership under extreme stress. Coordinated the actions of 40 students, 9 instructors, and 30 support personnel.
• Chosen to screen, select, and train 30 qualified Marines for the elite missions of reconnaissance and target acquisition.
• Conducted preparatory training which produced, on two occasions, the top two graduates of the Marine Corps' most demanding special school.
• Developed comprehensive training in land navigation, communications, and patrolling culminating in a week of unprecedented independent operations in the Mojave Desert.
• Co-developed original doctrine for cliff assaults, later adopted throughout the Marine Corps.

Organizational Management
• Coordinated the training schedules of a battalion's six subordinate companies.
• Scheduled and coordinated all training for the Marine Corps' first fully qualified raid force throughout a six-month deployment to the western Pacific.
• As Officer-in-Charge of a U. S. Marine Mobile Training Team, supervised weapons and tactics training of 200 Philippine Marines, Republic of the Philippines.

Research/Analysis/Writing/Editing
• Masters' theses: *Vietnam: Reporters and the My Lai Crisis of 1968; Rethinking and Reinforcement in NATO "After the Pact": US Strategies and the Atlantic Alliance.*
• As Historical Officer, researched and wrote an account of a battalion's training and deployment.
• Selected for year-long Honors program, Department of History, Ames College; thesis: *America in Vietnam 1945-1950: The Origins of an Incomplete War.*
• Delegate to Naval Academy Foreign Affairs Conference, 1987.

INTERNATIONAL EXPERIENCE
• Traveled extensively: 49 states, The Netherlands, Italy, Okinawa, Republic of the Philippines, Republic of Korea, People's Republic of China, and Hong Kong.
• Working knowledge of Portuguese and Russian.

INTERESTS
• Active in Representative Assembly, African-American Society, and the Colloquium on Nuclear Weapons and Arms Control, Ames College.

EMPLOYMENT SITUATION:

Russell had been on an excellent career track with all the right qualifiers—degrees, experience, promotion, and tenure—until his last assignment. Due to a management change he was ousted just thirteen months after starting with a new company. His objective was to find a similar position as soon as he could with comparable salary and responsibility.

Russell had never experienced failure in his career before. He had worked long hours, including weekends, and entertained clients as well. He equated termination with failure. His feelings of embarrassment about the termination required primary attention in order for him to be able to sell himself to the market.

STRATEGIES FOR SUCCESS:

Russell's resume turned out to be the key to his healing. The process of looking back and writing down the facts of his specific work accomplishments had an expansive effect on his outlook. The more he thought and wrote, the more the emotional trauma reduced its hold on him. He came to feel proud of his accomplishments and to see the "politics" of his most recent situation. Russell found that he was quite employable, and the market responded very positively to him.

COVER LETTER STATEMENTS:

Over the years I have built a very solid career ladder that was interrupted recently by an executive shake-up at the top. I am ready to bring my expertise to your management table, and look forward to a discussion with you early next month.

I'm setting up interviews in your area and will call you in a week to see if we can find a convenient time to meet during my visit, September 10–17.

CRITICAL VIEWPOINT:

Russell was direct about his situation in his cover letter, but he left out the details (to be covered in the interview). His resume shows outstanding accomplishments, and speaks for him in clear absolute terms.

(Second page covers his successful career growth from 1967 to 1988, giving special attention to his first big management job in 1982.)

RUSSELL FLANDERS
62 Butte Mill Road
Boulder, CO 80301
Home: (303) 555-7766
Office: (303) 555-8805

JB KANE COMPANY	General Plant Manager	1992–PRESENT

Reporting to the Vice-President of Worldwide Engineering and North America Manufacturing with direct responsibilities for 800 employees. Plant generates $600 M in sales annually. Significant accomplishments include:

• Prior to my arrival, this plant had received an "unsatisfactory" rating from an internal audit. Within six months, I established and implemented specific procedures that resulted in a "satisfactory" rating.

• Developed and implemented fixed/firm/flexible scheduling system utilizing Just-In-Time philosophy to reduce inventory from $48 M to $24 M.

• Established 24 cross-functional employee involvement teams. Through these teams, developed and implemented numerous improvements including: enhancement of cell concepts, inventory control, supplier quality, welding processes, and effective line balancing. All this resulted in significant improvements in product quality, a net reduction of 25% on assembly hours per unit, and an overall productivity improvement of 20%.

• Aggressively pursued and implemented cost reduction plans and ideas through negotiated material cost reductions, reduction in labor hours per unit, engineering changes, throughput, and flow improvements that resulted in a cost reduction in excess of $12 M.

ANCHOR TRUCKS, INC.	1988 - 1992
Plant Manager	1989 - 1992

Held full responsibility for the Greenwood Manufacturing Plant producing $600 M in heavy-duty trucks.

• Integrated and absorbed the workload from a closed plant and doubled production capacity of this plant with no interruption to production.

• Drove down hours to build unit by 35% which resulted in a 500% increase of plant profitability over three years.

M.S. in Industrial Engineering—University of Colorado
B.S. in Industrial Engineering—University of Pennsylvania

EMPLOYMENT SITUATION:

Louise was a fifty-three-year-old homemaker with extensive volunteer experience and concurrent but part-time paid work experience. She now wanted a full-time, professional position. She knew her volunteer credits were worthy but she was confused on how to package herself to compete.

STRATEGIES FOR SUCCESS:

Louise's counselor helped her put together a functional resume directed toward her job target of development and corporate giving. Louise's volunteer experience included admirable fundraising credits that she listed right at the top of her resume. Although she still held her unrelated part-time job at the time she wrote the resume, she listed it after her two major volunteer positions that were now ending.

COVER LETTER STATEMENTS:

At the recommendation of Harrison Schimker, I am forwarding my resume for the position of Development Director of the Arizona Light Opera Company.

My background in development work for Arizona State University has provided me with a variety of experiences in fundraising, including prospective donor and group presentations, event planning, membership drives, personal contact, cold-calling, and creation of print and media material. You'll see from my resume that I've worked with boards of directors, groups of volunteers, and a professional staff.

Having lived in Arizona for many years, I've been associated and involved with many facets of the community, including various arts and performing groups, academic and professional associations, and state commissions and foreign relations councils. My experience is compatible with the communication and administrative skills you desire.

CRITICAL VIEWPOINT:

Louise's resume was full of competitive results of which she could be proud. She also had a large network of influential contacts that could help her open doors. Her cover letter used the name of the Board Vice-President of the potential employer.

LOUISE FOLEY
17 Dorcas Circle East
Mesa, AZ 85206
(602) 555-2169

JOB TARGET: DEVELOPMENT AND CORPORATE GIVING

FUNDRAISING/DEVELOPMENT/SALES:
- Raised over $170,000 for the ASU School of Music during a ten-year period. Raised $20,000 for a single event this year.
- Increased retail sales for women's boutique by 32% as part-time employee. Was offered own store based on successful retail ability.
- Raised $65,000 in four months for high school band to perform in Fiji.
- Saved organization over $2,500 in insurance premiums through research.

EVENT PLANNING:
- Successfully developed and coordinated six golf tournaments.
- Planned and organized ten "friend-raising" events for ASU School of Music. Other universities used this successful group as a model for their development programs.
- Planned and organized membership and audience development campaigns for nonprofit arts organization.
- Oversaw and promoted various events via print and electronic media, including appearances and interviews.
- Served as President, Board of Directors, ASU Music Circle for two years, supervising 30 active volunteers.

MANAGING/SUPERVISING:
- Served as president of various community organizations, managing groups of volunteers in event and fundraising efforts.
- Served as President of Board of Trustees at church, supervising board of twelve.

SKILLS:
- Speaking Spanish.
- Public speaking.
- Writing and editing.
- Typing, computer literate and learning!

EXPERIENCE:
1988–1993	ARIZONA SCHOLARSHIPS FUND GOLF TOURNAMENT
	Assistant Chair
1983–1993	ASU MUSIC CIRCLE BOARD OF DIRECTORS
	President, 1984-1986
1991–present	FOLEY'S FASHION—Fashion consultant and sales
1989–1991	THE RITZ CLOTHING BAZAAR—Sales
1983–1988	EDITOR—ASU School of Music Newsletter

EDUCATION:
B.S. Cal State University
Workshops in public relations, writing, brochures, development
Spanish Language Certification, U. S./Mexico Institute, Mexico City
Undergraduate and graduate courses in music from Cal State University

EMPLOYMENT SITUATION:

At fifty-six David lost his job due to his company's merger with a larger firm that kept its own management team. He had had a long, successful work history with one company, but now he was on the market without a college degree, in a technical field dominated by engineers with advanced degrees. Although his severance package was excellent, David felt it was too soon to retire. He wanted to be back in action.

STRATEGIES FOR SUCCESS:

David's career advisor convinced him not to try to compete with younger Ph.D. engineers, but to market himself to executives of a similar age and background. His resume was organized by function, with management given primary focus on page one. David's personal network was broad, and helped him find several manufacturing companies that had succeeded with shirt-sleeve management. He targeted his campaign entirely at these executives.

COVER LETTER STATEMENTS:

As a result of the acquisition of my prior employer, I am identifying other companies in the region that could benefit from my experience and management skills.

For a number of years I fulfilled management responsibilities in purchasing and manufacturing operations for a Houston-based manufacturing company considered a leader in technological application and efficiency. As a result of that experience, I gained many valuable skills and abilities that I think will be useful to your firm. Some examples of my accomplishments include:

- Saved over $1.2M in acquisition costs through effective buying management.

- Established 'partnership' and 'total quality' programs with suppliers.

CRITICAL VIEWPOINT:

David's strategy worked for him. He was offered a position as a plant manager in a semi-related industry.

(Second page covers planning and purchasing, and education.)

DAVID B. FOLTZ
29 Woodland Haven Road
Houston, TX 77062
(703) 555-4017

EXPERIENCE: MAGELLAN MANUFACTURING, Houston, TX 1956–1992

A custom manufacturer of state-of-the-art combustion-related equipment for the hazardous waste–disposal and petrochemical industries.

Vice-President—Manufacturing	1992
Vice-President and Director—Manufacturing	1982–1992
Plant Manager	1956–1982

MANAGEMENT:

- Managed up to 35 departments and 600 employees.
- Team member and manufacturing liaison with data processing personnel on the implementation of MAPICS II and MicroData automated business systems.
- Initiated system that resulted in sizable reduction in controllable inventory along with quantitative system of measuring inventory related to work-in-process.
- Developed master job schedule that doubled on-time deliveries.
- Knowledgeable of both domestic and export shipping procedures.
- Assisted marketing in sales presentations from both a manufacturing and purchasing perspective.

MANUFACTURING:

- Instituted assembly line process for custom-designed and custom-built products resulting in a 40% reduction of assembly labor.
- With engineering, coordinated value analysis of Vapor Recovery System resulting in a 50% labor reduction.
- Assisted in start-up of an overseas manufacturing plant including staffing and training.
- Consolidated four machine operations into one dedicated machine operation resulting in a 60% reduction of labor costs.

PLANNING:

- Developed one-year and five-year manufacturing and purchasing plans from sales forecasts by product line.
- Prepared and approved departmental manpower, capital and expense budgets.

MILITARY   United States Army 1976–1978.
SERVICE   Captain—Honorable Discharge.

EMPLOYMENT SITUATION:

Louis was a minority member with over twenty-two years of combined employment and entrepreneurial experience. He had worked as a consultant, and as an officer in his own companies
and other firms. Through the years he had advised various businesses, private industries, and
governmental agencies.

After eighteen years of entrepreneurial activity, Louis was again seeking employment, and targeted various advertising and marketing firms.

STRATEGIES FOR SUCCESS:

Louis's primary challenge was making the transition from being his own boss to working for
someone else. In making initial contact with a potential employer it was essential for Louis to
convey a willingness to learn, adjust, and adapt to the procedures and philosophy of the company. This willingness was established first in his cover letter. With his counselor, he role-played
interviews to experience and communicate himself as someone who could help facilitate and enhance the growth and development of someone else's company. A positive attitude was key to
his success.

COVER LETTER STATEMENTS:

I am seeking opportunities with your firm as a Marketing/Advertising Manager. I would bring to
your organization over twenty-two years of experience, eighteen of which were as an entrepreneur in the marketing/advertising arena.

This is a competitive industry, and key personnel with strong histories of success in this business are long-term assets to your organization. I have such a background, and I am also willing
to learn and adapt to new and innovative approaches within the field. I am very result-oriented,
and I work at my best when I'm pushing to achieve a goal within an organization.

CRITICAL VIEWPOINT:

Louis was successful on all counts. His phone techniques, self-marketing letter, resume,
and interviewing skills all worked together to help him land a job as vice-president of marketing services with a local bank.

(Second page covers early work history and education.)

LOUIS H. FOSTER
14553 Milmarson Place, N.W.
Washington, DC 20011
(202) 555-4132

PRESIDENT
Louis H. Foster & Associates   Washington, D. C.   1983–present

Consulting, Program Management & Business Development
This consulting firm provides various sales, marketing, and promotional services to government,
business, industrial, and institutional agencies.
Researched, designed, and implemented contract compliance, economic development, training
and entrepreneurial/business programs in the following areas:
- Human Resource Management & Relations.
- Urban, Public, Community, & Consumer Affairs.
- Advertising & Public Relations.
- Minority Recruitment, Retention, Relations, and Program Development.

EXECUTIVE DIRECTOR   1979–1983
Department of Housing Policy/Development & Property Management
Catholic University   Washington, D.C.

Program Development, Planning, Management, Marketing & Promotions
Developed & managed a federal housing grant for the purpose of merging the academic and
business/professional sector. The development of a diverse and comprehensive curriculum
module and training program proved to be highly successful and benefited graduate and
undergraduate students.
- Developed supportive services (counseling, training, supervision, financing,
  management & development).
- Provided leadership and supervision for program development and coordination with
  highly skilled professional staff (finance committee, academicians, program developers,
  consultants, administrators, etc.).
- Interfaced with public/private sector housing professionals to benefit community
  development, social services, finance, security, and support systems.
- Coordinated the upgrading and acceptance of standard criterion requirements by HUD for
  the certification of public housing managers.
- Monitored program activity: quality control, budget expenditures, policy & procedures,
  business/community development.
- Nominated by the Dean of the School of Public and Urban Affairs as "Most Outstanding
  Businessman in the Nation."
- Worked in conjunction with the legislative and political process to develop funds for
  abandoned and deteriorating homes in major urban areas.

EXECUTIVE DIRECTOR/PRESIDENT   1976–1979
Housing Development & Loan Fund, Incorporated
Housing Development Division   Greenbelt, MD

Leadership, Program Development, Public Relations
As Executive Director and President for the Board of Directors, provided management, strategic
professional/technical leadership in the areas of research, lobbying, acquisition development,
marketing, and program feasibility for diverse housing programs. These programs were
directed to meeting the needs and goals of city-county government and the community.

EDUCATION:
City University of New York—Liberal Arts

EMPLOYMENT SITUATION:

Erica was three months away from receiving her degree when she came into counseling. She had had little paid work experience relative to her job target, and was concerned, like many recent graduates entering the full-time job market for the first time, that her nonpaid experience was too weak and irrelevant.

STRATEGIES FOR SUCCESS:

Organizing her resume was key in building Erica's confidence that she could present herself as a professional. Although Education is usually listed up front for a recent graduate, her counselor had her put it at the bottom since her degree was not in her chosen field of film and television. She separated Professional Experience from Employment History because her nonpaid work deserved high visibility on the page.

Erica tapped the network she had developed during her film and TV internship and her acting and modeling experience to obtain names of studio executives with whom to start her job campaign. With all the competition in the Los Angeles market, Erica knew she had to persist at making personal contacts, and not burn herself out cold-calling.

COVER LETTER STATEMENTS:

[To a Vice-President of Programming at Paramount Studios:]

Hal Goodleif at 20th Century Fox was kind enough to offer your name as that of someone who could help me identify current projects for which I might be suited as a production assistant.

My experience includes three production internships, as well as acting and modeling. I'm fully trained to accept responsiblity and work the long hours necessary to achieve an on-time, successful production deadline.

CRITICAL VIEWPOINT:

Erica's main job was to use the phone to make every possible contact. The job of production assistant commands very little money, but is a good place to start. There's lots of socializing in the Los Angeles market, so it was advisable for her to have a good business card and a notebook/address book always at hand, and a willingness to quickly follow up every lead.

ERICA SIMMS FRANK
50012 Loma Place
Los Angeles, CA 90026
(213) 555-8397

OBJECTIVE: PRODUCTION ASSISTANT IN FILM, TELEVISION, OR VIDEO

SUMMARY OF QUALIFICATIONS

- Knowledgeable about many aspects of media performance and production.
- Consistently recognized as having excellent interpersonal skills, and ability to work under pressure.
- Excellent oral and written communication skills developed through my education and work.
- Highly motivated to expand knowledge and skills in all aspects of media production/promotion.

PROFESSIONAL EXPERIENCE

COMMUNICATION/MEDIA PRODUCTION

- Three production internships (involving film, video and television)—Assisted in and observed entire production and editing process including a major television series, *The Young and the Restless*; assisted producers in coordinating and administering commercials; arranged casting calls; assisted talent; trained in budget control and bidding for commercials; logged, timed, corrected and typed scripts; created script synopses; assembled and distributed scripts.
- Acted—involving live audience performance for Twentieth Century Fox, extra work on television series: *Hunter, L.A. Law, It's a Living, Raymond Burr;* and in movies: *Fabulous Baker Boys, Gremlins II, Wizard, HarlemNights.*
- Modeled—involving poise and audience performance for Aspen Leaf, Fashion Bar, May D&F, J.M. Kenner, Water Pik, Pro Magazine; also ramp and photography model.

BUSINESS/MARKETING

- Produced and directed five video projects, including two for the college television channel.
- Organized a public relations campaign for a group research project.
- Active in sales, promotion, and customer service; complimented on excellent customer service.
- Trained new employees.
- Good telephone and general office skills.

EMPLOYMENT HISTORY
(Part-time while in school) 1988–present

Sales/Customer Service—(1991–present), Candy Factory	Los Angeles, CA.
Make-up Assistant—(1987–present), Beautiful Faces	Los Angeles, CA.
Extra—(1990–present), Twentieth Century Fox, Kerner/Koch, dick clark productions, Glorious Productions	Los Angeles, CA.
Catering Assistant—(1988–1992), Sands Point Catering	Redondo Beach, CA.
Model—(1985–present), J.A. Models Inc.	Brentwood, CA.

EDUCATION

University of California, Los Angeles, B.A. Communications (Graduating May 1993)
Minor: Business GPA 3.5–4.0; Dean's List

Relevant Course Work—Communications I&II, Public Relations, Journalism, Speech-Making, Research Methods, Marketing, Introduction to Business, Computer Literacy, Interpersonal Communication, Leadership, Persuasion, and Corporate Script Writing.

EMPLOYMENT SITUATION:

Constance worked for one large retail store for fifteen years. She felt stifled in her position there; she felt that her managers gave her little credit for her accomplishments, and they indicated that there was no more room for her to grow. She was looking to move up to international merchandising, where she could be high-powered and visible.

STRATEGIES FOR SUCCESS:

Fortunately Constance had saved records of her accomplishments over the last ten years. She was coached by her career counselor to show both the breadth and depth of her eighteen years' experience, and to position herself as a bottom-line, results-producing executive. The power of her past experience was easily communicated, and her resume was packed with impressive statistics.

Her vast personal network of international vendors, whose names and numbers she kept in her records, proved invaluable.

COVER LETTER STATEMENTS:

In almost twenty years as a retail management executive, I have dramatically increased sales and profits and developed new business. My leadership has spanned the following: market forecasting, inventory management, merchandising distribution, profit analysis, vendor negotiations, product development, promotional planning, training, image development, security control, systems, and product presentation.

I've been acknowledged as a successful strategist and innovator in turning around unprofitable ventures, as well as in designing efficiency measures and systems.

CRITICAL VIEWPOINT:

Constance's background was ideal for a one-page chronological resume: she's staying in the same field; she has had only one employer and sufficient promotions, and has lots of results that stand out.

CONSTANCE GARCIA
14 Carriage Lane
Saddle River, NJ 07458
(201) 555-8068

CAREER OBJECTIVE : INTERNATIONAL MERCHANDISING EXECUTIVE

1978–Present   **BIERBAUM & SONS,   NEW JERSEY DIVISION**
26 stores serving Mid-Atlantic States

1987–Present   **Merchandise Counsellor**
Men's Dress Shirts

- Senior merchandising executive reporting to Group Vice-President, supervising four buyers.
- Worked closely with international designers and manufacturers in London, Paris, Milan, Hong Kong and Singapore to develop new products.
- Increased sales volume 150%: $8M to $20M with a 216% increase in profit.
- Changed product mix through analysis of merchandise productivity and profitability.
- Developed new product-line vendor relations and negotiations resulting in higher profit margins.
- Designed and oversaw *in store* merchandising plans for all stores.
- Redirected inventory standards resulting in reduced shortages.
- Provided effective training for store personnel resulting in increased sales and team spirit.

1987   **Store Merchandise Manager**
Misses/Women's Sportswear, Juniors, Dresses,
Coats, Furniture, Housewares and Domestics

- Increased volume 25%/$15M to $20M compared to total store increase of 15%.
- Directed total concept thinking. Analyzed business and maximized sales through improved merchandise acquisition, elimination of slow-selling merchandise, optimal floor plans and effective training.

1984–1987   **Buyer**, Misses Designer/Updated Sportswear,
Handbags, Misses Sportswear, Maternity Wear

- Escalated sales from $4M to $9M and profit from -25% to +10% within one year (Updated Sportswear).
- Enhanced product development through international travel and exploration (Updated Sportswear).
- Developed volume from $2M to $3.5M and profit reflecting a 70% increase (Handbags).
- Operated highly successful import program; traveled extensively to Hong Kong, Korea, Manila, and Europe (Handbags).
- Directed volume increase of 30% from $2.3 to $3M producing a 43% profit increase (Misses Sportswear).
- Augmented annual volume 40% from $1M to $1.4M, producing a 43% profit increase (Maternity Wear).

EDUCATION   St. John's University,   B. S. Commerce / Marketing

EMPLOYMENT SITUATION:

Ray was a young man with less than ten years' work experience, all as a self-employed sales representative. He was now seeking a corporate sales position that would allow him to use his natural ability in sales, provide more security than he could count on from self-employment, and get him into an industry that was not suffering from the recession then at its peak. Although his sales track record was excellent, he had no corporate experience and would normally be considered difficult to market, especially in a recessionary economy.

STRATEGIES FOR SUCCESS:

Ray needed to emphasize his natural ability as a salesman, self-starter, producer, and leader among his peers—all qualities in demand by sales organizations. In an unusual presentation (an exception to the rule) on the counsel of his career advisor, Ray added a final word that demonstrated a highly supportive relationship between himself and his spouse. For a good sales rep to overcome the difficulties of constant rejection, this relationship is extremely important, and a good corporate sales manager understands this.

COVER LETTER STATEMENTS:

The most important aspect of my ability to sell is the ease with which I create relationships with people. I can bring these relationships to bear on your sales results, and so meet targets on a consistent basis.

My ability to sell in the difficult and currently depressed New England market is a clear demonstration of the results I can bring to your organization.

CRITICAL VIEWPOINT:

Ray's advantage in the job market is his constant practice at selling. His target companies were large and diversified so that he would have room to move into management.

RAYMOND I. GLASSMAN
1221 Orchard Hill Road
Boston, MA 02130
(201) 555-9205

1985–Present   SALES REPRESENTATIVE—SELF-EMPLOYED

- Sought out and represented leading manufacturers of women's accessories in moderate and higher price ranges and achieved sales volume of $1.7 million.

- Developed extensive experience in working with large accounts and participating in trade shows, market weeks, and other marketing activities.

- Provided full range of sales services including telemarketing, direct sales, helping customers obtain credit lines from manufacturers, leading in-store seminars, performing in-store servicing and stock counts, following up on order deliveries, and solving a wide variety of problems.

- Rented, designed, and maintained a dynamic, beautifully furnished and decorated, highly organized Boston showroom.

- Increased sales of a single product to IP Jenner from $16,000 to $350,000.

- Convinced Hospitality Hosts, Inc., to be their representative in New England. Opened 200 accounts and sold over $375,000 worth of product in the first year in a territory in which they had no accounts.

- Maintained a sales volume over $850,000 for Lowell Bros. & Co., Inc., the largest glove manufacturer in the country. Opened two new accounts for them that totaled 360 branch stores.

- Represented Heilbron, Inc., a major umbrella resource. Sold umbrellas to 60 new accounts in six months, exceeding the output of every other sales rep.

- Recognized niche opportunity in wholesale jewelry sales and created new business.

- Made extensive use of computers for marketing as well as business management.

- Contributed unusual time, energy, and financial resources beyond what is normally expected of a sales representative. Developed and maintained effective partnership with my wife in marketing and managing the business.

EDUCATION

1985   **BOSTON UNIVERSITY,** Boston, MA
B.A. Economics, Summa Cum Laude

EMPLOYMENT SITUATION:

Clifford worked in the public sector for twenty years. For the last eight years he developed after-hours investment work. Within the last year he decided to switch to full-time work as a private-sector analyst. Although his current job was secure, the planned change felt challenging and attractive.

STRATEGIES FOR SUCCESS:

Clifford undertook a standard, logical search: his potential employers would be investment bankers, money managers, and savings-and-loan managers. After an active series of third-party networking conversations, he discovered a wealthy family seeking a full-time portfolio manager.

COVER LETTER STATEMENTS:

Our mutual friend, Stanford Langley, suggested I contact you about your needs for a portfolio manager. The attached resume details my multiple skills and professional credentials.

I feel my previous affiliation with the health care and educational fields would be most useful to you. I have already made numerous trades in these two areas. I understand you have an investment philosophy that could make us a good match for each other.

I am discreet and efficient and have access to many investment relationships that could be fruitful to you as you expand your portfolio.

CRITICAL VIEWPOINT:

Clifford's resume very quietly disguises the bulk of his worklife as a public sector employee, although the facts and results of those years are fully accounted for. As you can see by his resume, Clifford was hired by this wealthy family. (This resume reflects his update *after* he was hired.)

CLIFFORD I. GLOVER
7831 Northridge Road
Lincoln, NE 68516
(w) (402) 555-4631
(h) (402) 555-1359

ANALYSIS:

- Developed a stock selection method that results in a projected return six times greater than the Dow Jones Industrial Average increase.
- Performed analyses which have produced stock selections that consistently achieved an above average return on a risk-adjusted basis.
- Analyzed numerous applications for funding including an evaluation of cost budgets and revenue projections.
- Produced monthly client newsletter containing "best bet" stock picks.
- Participated in research projects on the following topics:
    Effects of reduced institutionalism on the elderly.
    Method for reducing cultural barriers to cancer screening among Sioux Indians.
    Effects of Medicare on patterns of hospital utilization in five midwest communities.
- Author of three articles appearing in professional publications.
- Performed tax planning/preparation for investment accounts.

INVESTMENTS:

- Started and continue to manage an investment business composed of three major areas of concentration: limited partnerships, individual accounts, and newsletter clients.
- Series #7 license; associated with Grey Investments and Insurance.
- SEC licensed investment advisor.
- Managed trusts and personal accounts.

MANAGEMENT AND ADMINISTRATION:

- Chaired committee to develop a formula for determining nursing home bed need per geographic area.
- Qualified numerous areas to receive additional medical manpower.
- Administered National Health Service Corps contract.
- Chaired a task force to determine the type and usage of health data to be used by state and local agencies.
- Supervised clerical staff.

WORK HISTORY:

1990–Present	**Investment Manager**, Chadwick Enterprises, Lincoln, NE.
1985–Present	**Licensed Investment Advisor**, Clifford I. Glover Enterprises, Omaha, NE.
1978–1990	**Senior Health Planner**, State Health Planning and Development Agency, Division of Health Systems Planning, Omaha, NE.
1970–1977	**Research/Teaching Assistant** for University of Idaho

EDUCATION:

University of Nebraska, 1985, M.B.A.
University of Idaho, 1973, M.A. (Sociology)

EMPLOYMENT SITUATION:

Leslie was a former physical education teacher who successfully moved into health care, and also took a year in management consulting with a training organization. She liked working in new and challenging environments. She longed for a career in the film industry.

STRATEGIES FOR SUCCESS:

At the time she sought career advice, Leslie had no full-time or paid experience in film, and no education in TV or other media. She was seeking a total career change. Leslie's counselor had her enroll in acting classes and volunteer for every possible job in her chosen industry to gain credits that would be marketable and could be used on her resume. She gathered these volunteer experiences during her year as a consulting project manager for Career Builders, Inc.

COVER LETTER STATEMENTS:

As an assistant producer, I covered all aspects of television over a six-month period. The 'Health Talk' program was all my original work, including creating the concept, researching it, casting it, and being involved in every aspect of production. I also did script-writing and editing in pre-production.

I have worked with demanding people at the top of the industry, and am able to respond quickly to production needs with professionalism and quality.

CRITICAL VIEWPOINT:

Although in her mid-thirties competing with people in their early twenties, Leslie had the confidence to market herself aggressively in a field in which she needed hands-on experience to be able to open doors. Her year of volunteering was filled with eighteen-hour days, as she still needed full-time paid work in order to carry on with her life.

LESLIE GRANT
88 Guber Lane
Montclair, NJ 07042
(201) 555-9238

1992-Present   TELEVISION AND FILM PRODUCTION

TELEVISION:

"Sisterhood" LIFETIME Cable Network magazine format   **Associate Producer**
ALICE Awards (4); ACE nomination; Host: Linda Garner

"Ron Randall's SPORTSTIME" sports call-in show   **Director**
68 hour-long shows (live)

"Health Talk" 39 wrap-arounds, all networks   **Assistant Producer**

"Best of the Explorers" PBS Host: Bill Moyers   **Camera**
12 half-hour shows

"Holistic Approach" Cablevision Host: Jan Fender   **Camera**
31 half-hour shows

WSBC-54 Cablevision of Southern, NJ —all areas of production and technical operation

FILM:

Disney Production "Scenes from a Mall" (Mazursky)   **Assistant**
Assistant to Woody Allen and Bette Midler

Recorded Picture Company "Everybody Wins" (Reisz)   **Assistant**
Assistant to Film Editor (Winger/Nolte)

MGM/UA "Stanley and Iris" (Ritt) Fonda/DeNiro   **Assistant**
Assistant to Casting Director-background

DOCUMENTARY/ INDUSTRIAL: Specifics on request

PRIOR EXPERIENCE:

1991 -1992	CAREER BUILDERS, INC.	Consulting	New York, NY
1987 -1991	O.K. HEALTH-AID, INC.	Consultant	Staten Island, NY
1985 -1987	ANN HORACE MEDICAL CLINIC	Director of Geriatric Services	Montclair, NJ
1978 -1985	MONTCLAIR PUBLIC SCHOOLS	Department Coordinator	Montclair, NJ

EDUCATION:

Actors' Workshop —Warren Robertson   Acting Class—Uta Hagen
University of New Hampshire —completed MS Degree course work
Colgate University, BS

SPECIAL SKILLS:

Computer literacy, reflexology, driver's license, scriptwriting, research, photography, videography

EMPLOYMENT SITUATION:

Barry was a recent college graduate with a major in music and a minor in communications. Although he was a gifted concert violinist, his career goal was television broadcast writing and production, with sports his special interest. He had only volunteer experience in the area, but his credits were good.

STRATEGIES FOR SUCCESS:

Barry had many friends in broadcasting. He only needed to package himself for that business and to follow up a couple of serious leads. He insisted to his career counselor that the music background not be mentioned in his resume.

With the music major deleted, the communications minor was listed as if it were his major. Education was placed at the bottom, so that he could chronologically list his broadcast credits up front. The Production Assistant's job listed at the top was an unpaid summer position.

COVER LETTER STATEMENTS:

Jeff Sturgis, the new station manager at your sister affiliate in Roanoke, suggested I contact you. He mentioned some new start-up positions being discussed at your station.

My experience is diversified, with a short but strong work history in broadcasting. I learn quickly and consider myself extremely flexible. I have also been informally interviewing sports writers to clarify and improve my writing skills. I'm enclosing a short news article as a sample of my writing.

CRITICAL VIEWPOINT:

Barry could have included music on his resume. Given his youth, it could be perceived as an asset even to the most hard-nosed broadcasting executives. However, he preferred a total focus on his career target.

Ordinarily, a new graduate puts Education at the top of the resume, but in this case it would only highlight that the degree is not in broadcasting or television.

BARRY GREEN
41412 Penartin Road, S.W.
Roanoke, VA 22124
(703) 555-7392

JOB OBJECTIVE: BROADCAST WRITING and PRODUCTION

EXPERIENCE:

1993   HARDEE SPORTS NEWS NETWORK, Roanoke, VA
                Production Assistant

- Ensured that playback technicians followed precise orders of producers/directors.
- Managed responsibilities for all incoming feeds; coordinated with show producer and assigned events to editors for logging and editing.
- Edited game tapes for broadcast and wrote accompanying script. Logged various sports events.
- Operated and programmed Odetics TCS 2000 Commercial Coordinator. Loaded and ran tapes for broadcast.

1991-1993   WGMU 540AM/BROADSIDE GEO. MASON UNIVERSITY, Fairfax, VA
                Sportscaster/Disc Jockey/Sports Writer

- Wrote, edited and broadcasted local/national sports news for two-minute time spots twice weekly.
- Programmed and presented rock music for three-hour show. Reported local, national and international news/weather.
- Contributed articles pertaining to both athletic events and participants in the GMU sports program.

1991-1992   WGBM BUSINESS RADIO 1430, Greenbelt, MD
                Intern

- Assisted News Director in gathering, editing and writing news.
- Arranged and conducted interviews with newsworthy people.
- Edited sound bytes for broadcast.
- Taught new employees operation of program board.

EDUCATION: George Mason University B.A. Communications/English Writing   1993

EMPLOYMENT SITUATION:

Randy was a recent college graduate with only part-time paid work experience. His drinking problems landed him in an alcohol treatment facility a month after he graduated from college, and he was under care for mental illness. He was active in a volunteer outpatient recovery program which supported him in seeking full-time employment.

STRATEGIES FOR SUCCESS:

Randy was referred to a career counselor by the hospital at which he'd been treated. It was recommended that he apply for an entry-level position at a social service agency and work toward a master's degree. He decided not to hide his past alcoholism and mental illness. Although he was on medication for depression, he functioned normally as long as he followed his prescribed regime. He focused in his job search on social service agencies that would perceive his personal experiences as contributing to what he could offer on this job.

Randy prepared a targeted resume, as he was selling capability and willingness more than direct work experience.

COVER LETTER STATEMENTS:

Since I have first-hand experience in fighting back from mental illness, I am uniquely qualified to understand your clients. I also offer good administrative skills that I developed during my undergraduate student days, including the ability to work through government procedures and forms.

CRITICAL VIEWPOINT:

Although there is new legislation protecting the rights of the mentally ill in the workplace, Randy is still taking a risk by divulging his history in a cover letter. Given his chosen employer target, however, it is probably a risk worth taking. In an ordinary business setting, outside of social services, he might be well-advised to be more discreet.

RANDALL M. HARRINGTON
72415 Appian Way
Chattanooga, TN 37415
(615) 555-4266

JOB TARGET: ADMINISTRATIVE ASSISTANT—SOCIAL SERVICES

EDUCATION: B.A. Sociology/Political Science
DREXEL UNIVERSITY   Philadelphia, PA   1992

CAPABILITIES:

- Good analytic and planning skills.
- Work independently and as a team member.
- Clerical abilities ranging from typing 70 wpm to fast notehand.
- Able to show compassion and understanding.
- Work with patience and focus under pressure.
- Good telephone manner.
- Work well with statistics and complex reports.

ACHIEVEMENTS:

- Completed 600 five-page data collection forms for the U.S. Census Bureau in 45 days.
- Handled cash receipts and customer sales for a small retail shop.
- Collected and analyzed data for a U.S. presidential campaign headquarters.
- Assisted in all clerical duties of a presidential campaign headquarters.
- Canvassed 1000 homes over a 60-day period.
- Aided a human rights organization in focusing public policy through letter-writing and issues education.
- Assisted this organization in fundraising activities and petition campaigns.

WORK EXPERIENCE:

1992	U.S. Presidential Campaign Howard Davies	Clerk
1991	Amnesty International	Clerk
1991	Armco Oil and Gas (summer)	Attendant
1990	U.S. Census Bureau (spring)	Administrative Assistant
1989	St. John's Lutheran Church	Maintenance
1987-88	Aggie's Sweet Tooth Shoppe	Salesperson

EMPLOYMENT SITUATION:

Rachel was changing her career from public relations writer to therapist. Her relevant work experience in counseling and therapy included only part-time or volunteer work, but her eight-year work history in public relations demonstrated she had already attained maturity in the workplace.

STRATEGIES FOR SUCCESS:

Rachel's career advisor had her do extensive research to help her focus on specific employer targets. The primary group she targeted needed multiskilled people who could handle family, individual, and group therapy. Rachel put together a functional resume to focus on those qualities she knew to be most needed. She added *Results* as a separate item under each function, as these are usually difficult to pinpoint in psychotherapy. Her part-time counseling and full-time public relations experience were listed under separate headings on the second page.

COVER LETTER STATEMENTS:

I enclose my resume in response to your recent advertisement for a therapist with a master's degree and background in family therapy. My credentials strongly support my application for this position.

YOUR NEEDS	MY BACKGROUND
M.A. Counseling	M.A. Counseling, U of Michigan, 1992
Background in family therapy	Employed a variety of family therapy techniques with families in crisis.
Treatment of individuals	Counseled in a variety of issues such as substance abuse, child abuse, and spouse abuse.

CRITICAL VIEWPOINT:

Her counselor guided Rachel well toward her targeted employers. Rachel generated many interviews and received praise for her resume, particularly the *Results* section.

(Second page covers her work history, education, and awards, and lists her counseling as professional experience.)

RACHEL M. HEALY
7552 Tillman Place
Wilmington, DE 19801
(302) 555-5463

JOB OBJECTIVE:	Professional therapist, using skills and knowledge in various therapeutic modalities, as well as written and oral communications.

ACHIEVEMENTS:

Family Therapy

Provided family therapy to families in crisis in major medical facilities, educational institutions, and family service agencies. Employed techniques emphasizing creativity and flexibility, such as joining, modeling, educating, reframing, and therapeutic paradox.

Results: Supervisor comments: *"Proved to be imaginative, responsible, exceptionally motivated, sensitive ... excellent at making connections in the big picture."*

Individual Therapy

Provided individual counseling at various agencies. Proficient with wide range of therapeutic modalities.

Results: Effectively counseled "difficult" clients by using skills from many fields including substance abuse therapy. Supervisors consistently commented: *"High promise ... best we've had in the position ... bright and resourceful ... a pleasure to know and to work with."*

Group Therapy

Provided group therapy in a variety of settings including major medical facilities, educational institutions, and family services agencies. Employed systems approach to facilitate clients with issues such as death, divorce, and child abuse.

Results: Comments from reviews: *"Good insight ... overall quality of these sessions superb ... quick to establish trust and rapport."*

Verbal and Written Communications

Prepared accurate, clear, and timely reports.
Handled correspondence between clients and agencies.
Administered $90,000 grant to create educational and marketing materials and to document their effect on attitude change.
Developed education presentations and programs.

Results: Commendation for invaluable contribution and *excellence of work* from Governor's Advisory Board; awards for *excellence* in television public service. Consistently received superior ratings for quality of work. Client commented: *"I was moved by her presentation; now I know where to go for help."*

Outstanding Young Women of America—1990.

EMPLOYMENT SITUATION:

Terry had a long and diverse work history in psychotherapy, counseling, and rehabilitation therapy. She was seeking a long-term, secure position in an institutional setting that would provide her with the stability and professional challenge appropriate to her experience and abilities. Problems in her work history included several unsuccessful forays into private practice, gaps due to intermittent educational experience, and only one job that lasted more than two years.

STRATEGIES FOR SUCCESS:

Terry's counselor suggested a functional resume that provided clarity about the range and depth of her experience without revealing the problems described above. Psychotherapy was chosen as her prime function because the breadth of the field increased the probability of her finding a suitable position. Rehabilitation therapy was included to demonstrate Terry's ability to handle a technical discipline with expertise, but it was not emphasized. In both the counseling and rehabilitation therapy functions, supervisory/teaching experience was included.

COVER LETTER STATEMENTS:

The enclosed resume details the wide range and depth of my clinical experience. I can bring both special technical expertise and an understanding of people and their critical issues to your community clinic.

By combining my experience in private practice and extensive clinical work, I can provide your patients with the knowledge and understanding of their problems that will increase their self-confidence and inspire their loyalty to your clinic.

CRITICAL VIEWPOINT:

Terry broke tradition within her profession by avoiding the chronological format, as it would not have served her objectives. Her resume eliminated any possible confusion about her diverse experience by using the functional format.

TERRY HOLSAPPLE, C.S.W.
P. O. Box 4721
Woodstock, NY 12498
(914) 555-8503

PSYCHOTHERAPY
- Treated diverse outpatient population with various psychiatric disorders and physical disabilities.
- Treated clients with wide range of modalities.
- Practiced long-term and short-term individual psychotherapy using supportive, psychodynamic, and cognitive approaches.
- Practiced family and couples therapy.
- Delivered assertiveness group therapy.
- Practiced pain and stress management therapy.

COUNSELING
- Performed intake interviews including psychosocial assessments and treatment plans.
- Participated in interdisciplinary case conferences.
- Practiced crisis intervention and client advocacy.
- Supervised social work interns.

REHABILITATION THERAPY
- Performed audiologic evaluations and aural rehabilitation.
- Managed audiology services for diverse pediatric and adult population.
- Performed diagnostic evaluations and speech and language therapy.
- Coordinated Columbia University Master's Degree student practicum program at the Speech and Hearing Institute of ICD.

WORK HISTORY:

1993–Present	Private Psychotherapy Practice	Kingston, NY
1988–1993	International Center for the Disabled (ICD)	New York, NY
1991–1993	Senior Social Worker	
1988–1991	Staff Social Worker	
1989–1993	Private Psychotherapy Practice	New York, NY
1985–1987	New School for Social Research	New York, NY
	Clinical Audiologist	
1976–1985	Wide range of clinical therapeutic work and university teaching.	

EDUCATION:

1988	Columbia University School of Social Work	New York, NY
	M.S.W. in Clinical Social Work	
1975	Cornell University	Ithaca, NY
	M.S. in Speech Pathology and Audiology	
1973	Boston University	Boston, MA
	B.S. in Child Development and Family Relationships	

AFFILIATIONS AND CERTIFICATIONS:

New York State Social Work Certification
National Association of Social Workers
ASHA Certification in Speech Pathology and Audiology

EMPLOYMENT SITUATION:

Nels' background is typical of a professional-level classical musician with a wide range of skills and performances to his credit. His education is also typical, as it includes both university experience and private studies. He was seeking a permanent university position that would allow him to practice as a principal choral conductor. His lack of extensive teaching credentials or a Ph.D. was an obstacle.

STRATEGIES FOR SUCCESS:

Nels' counselor encouraged him to make a strong case for his broad experience as a conductor, the depth of his musical education, and his ability to work with a wide range of musical styles and repertoires including classical, barbershop, jazz, Broadway, and pop. The dense appearance of the resume, not usually recommended and difficult to read, was used here to visually emphasize Nels' extensive experience.

COVER LETTER STATEMENTS:

The broad range and depth of my musical experience can bring a flair and excitement to your classroom and to your regional public that will enhance the image of the university's cultural resources.

I can expand attendance at university concerts by the creation of an outstanding choral group and the development of a varied and interesting repertoire that will attract a broad segment of the public.

My extensive work as a professional choral and orchestral conductor and as a performer will add to the range of musical experience in your department and help to attract the very best students.

CRITICAL VIEWPOINT:

There is an overwhelming amount of detail, including names of individual teachers, but the few employers to whom Nels was applying would recognize those names. This resume represents a person in a very closed market. Hence, we allow the excess as an exception to the general rule. Nels won the position of choral conductor at a major university in the San Francisco Bay area.

NELS C. HOWLAND
726 El Hablo Street
Berkeley, CA 94750
(415) 555-6201

PROFESSIONAL EXPERIENCE:

Choral Conducting

- Conduct *Cable Car Chorus*, San Francisco's chapter of the Society for the Preservation and Encouragement of Barber Shop Quartet Singing in America (1991-Present).
- Conductor of the *Berkeley Singers*, a community mixed chorus of 20 to 30 voices with repertoire split evenly between "classical" and modern American music including Jazz, Broadway, and Pop (1986-Present).
- Conductor of the *Vocal Minority*, a select 16-voice mixed chorus specializing in Jazz, Broadway, and Pop (1984-Present).
- Prepared male chorus for performance of Brahms' *Alto Rhapsody* with the SFSU Symphony Orchestra, Lazlo Segan, Conductor (Spring, 1991).
- Prepared SFSU Chorus for performances with the SFSU Symphony of Beethoven's Ninth Symphony, Bach's Cantata #141, *Wachet auf! Ruft uns die Stimme*, and *Missa Brevis*, and Faure's *Requiem Mass* (1988-1989).

Orchestral Conducting

- Prepared and conducted SFSU Chamber Singers and Chamber Orchestra in West Coast premiere of John Rutter's *Requiem* (1990).
- Worked as Assistant Music Director for SFSU School of Creative Arts production of Andrew Lloyd Webber's *Evita* (Spring, 1989).
- Led on-stage orchestra in The Company's production of *Marat/Sade*, Stanford Memorial Church (1972).

Performance

- Accompanied voice and instrumental majors for SFSU Music Department (Fall, 1991).
- Served as Accompanist/Musical Director for a number of cabaret performers in venues ranging from the Plush Room and the On-Broadway to Fanny's and Chez Jacques (1982-1984).
- Accompanied Stanford University Chorus, Harold Jaspers, Conductor, during which time I worked with Maestros Josef Smith and Hans Hanover-Isserstol (1970-1972).

PROFESSIONAL MUSICAL EDUCATION:

Conducting

- Studied with Howard Eichenberger at the University of Southern California (Summer, 1991) and with the renowned conductor Paul Sataovonich at American Choral Directors Association Summer Conferences (1990 and 1991).

Vocal

- Studied privately for two years with Janette Moss; for three semesters with Sam Holsome; and with Dr. Brian Garry. Studied Lyric Diction and Vocal Pedagogy with Professor Curtwood Smith.

UNIVERSITY EDUCATION:

1991	**San Francisco State University**	Master's of Music
1973	**Stanford University**	Bachelor's Degree—Philosophy

PROFESSIONAL AFFILIATIONS:

- Member, American Choral Directors Association (ACDA)
- Member, Music Educators National Conference (MENC)

EMPLOYMENT SITUATION:

Carl wanted to upgrade his current university position to that of an academic counselor or financial aid advisor. His background was in quality assurance, equipment procurement, and aircraft mechanics. He had no direct experience, skills, or training in financial aid. He wanted a midlife career change, while continuing to work in a university setting.

Carl's unrelated work history and lack of education and training in the new field were considerable challenges to making this change.

STRATEGIES FOR SUCCESS:

Carl sought advice in investigating the two careers of academic counseling and financial aid counseling. His strong procurement background seemed translatable to the financial aid arena, but academic advising was a more difficult match for him. His career counselor suggested he emphasize the counseling skills he utilized when he advised high school students on career options in the U.S. Army. At the same time, Carl also volunteered in a local high school to help students and parents apply for college loans.

COVER LETTER STATEMENTS:

[This is an internal letter to another department at the university.]

I currently have over five years of work experience on this campus, and have interfaced with many departments, becoming familiar with their operations. My present work is in procurement, which offers several related applications to the position I am seeking. I spend considerable time advising personnel on the equipment most suitable to their needs.

My prior work experience includes counseling high school students concerning career opportunities with the U.S. Army, an activity that gave me good experience in working with a student population.

CRITICAL VIEWPOINT:

Carl would have done well with a functional or targeted resume, but he felt comfortable with a chronological format. He placed his volunteer experience at the top to increase his marketability in the framework of financial aid.

CARL JACKSON
19 Holly Hock Road
South Bend, Indiana 46637
(317) 555-2026 (W)
(317) 555-6455 (H)

CAREER OBJECTIVE: FINANCIAL AID ADVISOR

VOLUNTEER EXPERIENCE

WESTBROOK HIGH SCHOOL   1992–Present
Financial Aid Volunteer
  • Assist parents and students with college financial applications and banking relationships.

PROFESSIONAL EXPERIENCE

NOTRE DAME UNIVERSITY, South Bend, Indiana   1988–Present
Warehouse Coordinator
  • Responsible for surplus equipment for the University and three hospitals associated with the ND
    Medical Center, with equipment inventory of $800,000.
  • Coordinate "open and closed bid" sales and auctions on a regular basis to liquidate inventory.
    Proceeds amount to $200,000 annually.

FORT BENJAMIN HARRISON, Indianapolis, Indiana   1987–1988
Fleet Manager & Warehouse Supervisor
Forwarded military support elements for the Special Olympic Games.
  • Researched prices, contacted vendors, and made vendor recommendations
    concerning equipment procurement.
  • Coordinated delivery and pickup of equipment between civilian and military personnel.
  • Designed blueprints and specifications for a 15,000 s.f. warehouse and an 8500 s.f. kennel.
  • Ensured proper compliance of government contracts.
  • Scheduled daily use of 76 military vehicles and scheduled required maintenance.
  • Monitored vehicle millage and use to assure project budget did not exceed $500,000.
  • Supervised 20 people daily.

UNITED STATES ARMY   1984–1987
Maintenance/Supply Coordinator
Philippines and WV bases
  • Provided technical assistance concerning aircraft parts.
  • Researched manuals and other sources to locate suitable replacement parts and materials.
  • Served as liaison between maintenance and supply personnel.
  • Supervised 10-15 aircraft mechanics and supply personnel daily.

UNITED STATES ARMY   1964–1984
Maintenance/Material Control Supervisor
WV and Worldwide Army Bases
  • Advised and counseled high school students on career opportunities in the United States Army.
  • Directed scheduled and unscheduled maintenance for 24 aircraft.
  • Provided support to pilots concerning aircraft readiness.
  • Authorized aircraft's safety for flight.
  • Supervised 8 people daily.

EDUCATION

NOTRE DAME UNIVERSITY, South Bend, IN
  Bachelor of General Studies degree—Concentration: Government Procurement. December, 1992.
  GPA 3.32/4.0

EMPLOYMENT SITUATION:

After seven years with a major western U.S. bank, Roger lost his job in a merger with a southern bank. He had held three different middle management positions within the same bank, and he didn't want to leave the industry or his hometown. At the same time many other banks were suffering mergers and lay-offs.

STRATEGIES FOR SUCCESS:

Roger's bank provided him with an office, phone, administrative help, and outplacement counseling. The counselor helped him differentiate his experience from that of other bankers by highlighting the variety and breadth of his accomplishments. To be considered for jobs outside of banking, he listed his ability to handle a variety of financial questions and his computer skills separately.

COVER LETTER STATEMENTS:

[To a third-party contact:]

Our bank is merging in 120 days and relocating staff to North Carolina, but I have opted to stay in Las Vegas. My roots are here, and I feel committed to the community and to the local banking industry. I want to see Las Vegas continue to grow even though times are tough.

My career has been rich and full since joining Global. From my research, I understand you will be expanding your financial consulting division in coming months. I'd like to arrange a short meeting with you to review my credentials, so that if there's a near-term opportunity with your bank, I'll be available to join the effort.

CRITICAL VIEWPOINT:

Roger's resume presents his duties and accomplishments in a way that emphasizes his ability to produce tangible results, recognizing that in a competitive economy there is a premium on value added. He put a strong emphasis on research to find out about where his local banks were going. Given a relatively confined market, this was more necessary than ever.

(Second page covers the first two years at Global, education, and computer training.)

ROGER M. KELLEY
4915 North Durango Way
Las Vegas, NV 89129
(702) 555-6703

GLOBAL BANK OF AMERICA Las Vegas, NV   1986–1993

GLOBAL INVESTMENT BANKING Corporate Finance Associate

Participated in all facets of corporate finance within team-oriented
environment including valuations, mergers and acquisitions, and private
placement financings. Responsible for financial modeling, industry- and
company-specific offering memorandums, and various research projects.

Transactions participated in:
- Valuation and sale of medium-sized Nevada consumer finance
  company. Negotiated with high-level potential buyers.
- Negotiated sale of plant for large Nevada utility through
  leveraged-lease transaction. Created model to determine lease income
  stream and potential value.
- Valuation of all business units of major U.S. retailer representing
  important Global relationship. Results were presented to company
  management in order to illustrate company's need to reorganize.
- Financial advisor to major supplier of Taco Bell Restaurants.
  Financing needs assessment and financial modeling completed in
  order to contact potential investor in private placement, to be used for
  corporate expansion.

GLOBAL FINANCIAL CONSULTING Financial Consultant

Established new business unit for developing financial plans and financial
models for middle-market corporate customers. Developed and marketed
product. Within six months completed initial transaction. Department
increased from two to eight complements and to $250,000 in income within
three years. Performed financial modeling, financial plan memorandums,
graphics presentations, and oral presentations.

- Coordinated financial plan for profitable environmental engineering
  firm; Global increased working capital financing as a result of
  consulting study.
- Created computer-based financial model for large cigarette and candy
  distributor which was used internally by company for individual
  business units' budgeting process.
- Serviced over 150 of Global's middle-market customers.

- Sanstone's FinanSeer corporate finance analysis software
- ALCAR corporate finance package

EMPLOYMENT SITUATION:

Patricia suffered a serious head injury in an auto accident, and after two years of full-time recovery, she was able to work only part-time. She required an allergy-free, chemical-free environment, as even fluids from copy machines could affect her concentration. She was well educated and well traveled, a "super-salesperson," and wanted to stay at the same income level as before her accident. In addition, her savings were almost depleted after two years of unemployment.

STRATEGIES FOR SUCCESS:

Patricia's career counselor guided her first to a psychotherapist to help her cope with her disability. She was terrified of interviewing for fear of appearing weak or incapable. In addition, she had to adjust her "super-salesperson" self-image to accept a quieter, less time-consuming workstyle. Her counselor suggested a functional resume emphasizing titles and her diverse skills and accomplishments within her industry. She listed Real Estate Investor as her most recent job, although she had made only one investment during her two-year recovery.

COVER LETTER STATEMENTS:

I am a real estate sales agent with ten years' experience and a track record of accomplishments in commercial and residential leasing, sales, property management, and investing. I understand all levels of the market, and can relate well to the buying public.

CRITICAL VIEWPOINT:

In cases of persons with disabilities, full personal acceptance is absolutely necessary prior to launching a job campaign. In Patricia's case she will have to promote her highest skills during her interviews. When it's clear that a potential employer is ready to hire her, she must then be very precise and frank about her additional requirements. With an open mind and no apology, Patricia can negotiate her job needs to work well for her.

PATRICIA EILEEN KENT
2621 Ocean Avenue
Marina del Rey, CA 90272
(213) 555-4906

REAL ESTATE EXPERIENCE:

PROPERTY MANAGER

- Operated a 28-unit commercial complex and managed 175 residential luxury units.
- Managed all facets of marketing, advertising, maintenance, tenant selection and eviction.
- Drafted and negotiated commercial and residential leases, purchase and sale agreements.
- Directed and coordinated all activities of six staff members.
- Developed innovative marketing techniques which doubled profits in a two-year period and attracted a celebrity clientele.

NEW HOME SALES AGENT

- Coordinated arrangements for various housing tract developments, cooperating with builders and financial institutions from time of title search to closing.
- Sold 28 condos in three months for United Federal Savings and Loan and 19 homes within two weeks for development.
- Trained by Century 21.
- Handled all real estate expenses in a 90/10 commission split with broker.
- Appraised, marketed, sold, and arranged financing for private homes.
- Consistently met goal of a minimum two listings and one sale every month.

INVESTOR

- Negotiated the purchase of a triplex, vacant land, and three residences.
- Single-handedly renovated and resold properties for approximately 30-35% profit.

OTHER EXPERIENCES:

TEACHER/WORLD TRAVELER

- Wrote curriculum for successful model kindergarten program adopted by the State of Idaho.
- Taught kindergarten and third grade in inner city schools.
- Obtained an average three-year reading gain within one year.
- Individualized instruction in math and English which improved students' successes, motivating 35 potential high school dropouts to graduate.
- Traveled independently and extensively throughout the United States and eight European countries. Experienced various customs and cultures.

WORK HISTORY:

1991–1993	**Real Estate Investor**, Marina del Ray, CA
1988–1991	**Real Estate Sales**, Shaker Co.; Fairview Savings & Loan, Boise, ID
1985–1987	**Realtor/Property Manager**, Cyprus Properties, Sun Valley, ID
1982–1985	**Teacher**, Sandstone High, Sun Valley, ID
1980–1982	**Residential Realtor**, Century 21 / Steve Capp & Assoc., Boise, ID
1979–1980	**Teacher**, Boise Independent School System

EDUCATION: M.A., Education, University of Idaho

EMPLOYMENT SITUATION:

Garth was a senior executive at a Fortune 100 Company who lost his position through a merger and subsequent reorganization. He needed to project a strong image and solid record of results, and avoid projecting the hostile feelings arising from his sudden unemployment. He had seven children between the ages of 8 and 17, several of whom were nearing college age. Obviously he needed to find employment quickly.

Although company officials of the new regime were cordial, Garth was denied access to his office and to specific data from which to create an accurate resume.

STRATEGIES FOR SUCCESS:

Garth was upset and angry, and used several counseling sessions to vent his anger. He was able to work out his value statements for the resume at home and to write a powerful strategic marketing letter which emphasized his strengths as a sales executive. The resume stated his considerable accomplishments on one page.

COVER LETTER STATEMENTS:

As a professional executive for two Fortune 100 companies in the past 29 years, I have weathered every conceivable corporate storm, including an abrupt job loss due to a complex merger and a subsequent reorganization. My accomplishments are highlighted in the accompanying resume; however, the fine detail of my executive management eludes the best of resumes and requires a personal meeting.

CRITICAL VIEWPOINT:

Garth's cover letter is bold and speaks as one executive to another. His resume stands well on its own in a good one-page chronological format.

Notice that the bulk of information concerns the last ten years. Everything before then is given minimal exposure. He was clearly on a rising star—a perfect match for the chronological resume.

GARTH KITSOS
41 Old Hickory Lane
Princeton, NJ 08504
(609) 555-3460

1973–Present   **ADAMSBORO INDUSTRIES**   Princeton, NJ

1982–Present   **Vice President, Marketing Services**

- Instituted change in Consumer Division pricing policies resulting in company reaffirmation as industry leader.
- Revitalized sales organization and restructured field operations reducing expenses $1.15M and increasing sales $8.2M.
- Established effective communication strategy among all corporate departments eliminating redundancy, and influencing organizational effectiveness.
- Initiated distribution methods study saving $845K and improving customer services.
- Coordinated facilities relocation and incorporated automated and computer-assisted materials handling system, saving company $3.1M.
- Implemented computerized electronic system allowing accounts to order directly via on-site terminals.
- Restructured company graphics division reducing expenses by $410K.
- Redirected educational department emphasis to serve wider populations involving direct accounts as well as institutions.
- Chaired weekly meetings to interface effectively with all corporate divisions, resulting in dramatic improvement of internal communications.

1973–1982   **Sales Controller**

- Realigned company into appropriate divisions; analyzed allocated expenses into P and L responsibility.

1964–1973   **GENERAL SYSTEMS CORPORATION**   New York, NY
             Controller—International Division
- Established accounting system for 62 foreign franchises.

PROFESSIONAL AFFILIATIONS :

- American Management Club   •Sales Executive Club (SEC)

EDUCATION :   B.B.A. / Business Administration, Hofstra University

- Professional seminars/training in: sales, management, retail, computer technology

EMPLOYMENT SITUATION:

Adam was a super-bright high school graduate who started working in a gas station full-time at age eighteen. He never went on to college or sought any additional education. His job was busy and demanding. The gas station expanded to a major truck stop with many facilities, and within seven years he became General Manager. Ten years later, the truck stop was sold, and the new owner brought in his own staff, including a new General Manager.

STRATEGIES FOR SUCCESS:

Uncertain about what he wanted to do next, Adam sought a career advisor. He knew he was a good manager because people liked what he did but he also had no job-search experience. In the six months before the sale closed, Adam used every minute to educate himself as to his own capabilities. His resume was organized chronologically to display his outstanding career growth within one company. He directed it to a major competitor of the firm that had bought out his former employer.

COVER LETTER STATEMENTS:

I understand you'll be adding four new truck stops along Route 101 in the next eighteen months. Although you have a good reputation for promoting from within your own enterprise, I want to offer myself as the most competent, competitive outsider you could hire. My current employer has sold our location, and the new owner is bringing in his own staff. I am available anytime to take a new position, but can stay on here for another few months if I wish.

CRITICAL VIEWPOINT:

Adam's resume is loaded with powerful statements. He's fortunate because he likes what he's doing and his industry is still strong. His steady growth over seventeen years overshadows his lack of formal education beyond high school. Although it is highly unusual for a worker at this level to use a resume, both Adam's and his counselor's efforts paid off. A new job was secured within thirty days, which quickly led to a promotion.

ADAM L. KOCH
6331 Pine Crest Road
Carlsbad, CA 92009
(619) 555-5974

WORK HISTORY:

1976–present	Big 10 Truck Stop , New City, CA
1983–present	**General Manager**
1976–1983	Progressed from Fuel Island Attendant to General Manager

RESPONSIBILITIES:

- Hire, train, and direct the effort of up to 20 full- and part-time island and store employees.
- Manage inventory control of fuels, lubricants, accessories, and all convenience food items.
- Arrange product purchases and review purchase agreements with suppliers.
- Develop and implement a range of marketing operations.
- Oversee the preparation of all daily sales and inventory reports.
- Reconcile end-of-month reports.
- Manage account reconciliation, collections, and resolution of payment problems.
- Oversee property maintenance including electricity, plumbing, carpentry, and asphalt and concrete repair.

ACCOMPLISHMENTS:

- Based on the company's profitability, received as much as 35% of gross salary in annual bonus.
- Developed employee training programs which reduced equipment down-time, increased efficiency and improved customer service.
- Recommended, investigated, arranged for the purchase of, and coordinated the installation of new computer cash registers and island fuel pumps. This eliminated close to $30,000 annually in customer and employee theft.
- Redesigned and installed all point-of-sale shelving and displays within a very limited budget. This contributed to maintaining sales within a declining economy.
- Solicited and reviewed new credit card sales agreements. Trimmed credit card processing costs by 12%.
- Initiated new check approval system involving the collection of returned checks by outside company; reduced uncollectible checks by 95%, and reduced annual losses by approximately $28,000.
- Initiated and implemented a new program for the delivery of sister company products to customers. Placed the sister company in a more competitive position and increased gross sales.
- Frequently hire "first-time employees" and achieve average longevity of 18 months.
- Develop high staff morale. Out of 60 potential sick days available to employees, typically only 10 are used. Consistently fill Saturday work schedules with employees who volunteer to work the extra day.

EDUCATION: High School Graduate

EMPLOYMENT SITUATION:

Chris, a recent college graduate, had little interest in the trucking industry or in his unsatisfying position. He wanted a more traditional management position, but felt handicapped by his lack of a business degree—the same issue had made his initial job search difficult and impelled him to accept his current position. It was time for Chris to move on.

STRATEGIES FOR SUCCESS:

The targeted resume format was ideal for Chris's situation. It emphasized both his accomplishments and the foundations he had laid for a materials management position, a career objective he had researched and with which he felt comfortable. In the Capabilities section he listed the basic skills he had acquired in his current position that his research indicated would be assets in his target job.

COVER LETTER STATEMENTS:

I am conscientious in my personal and professional life. I take pride in myself and my work, and derive considerable satisfaction from doing an assignment well. I cope well with high-stress situations and can manage a variety of projects simultaneously. My specific proficiencies include excellent administrative and organizational skills, an ability to work tactfully with a variety of people and to learn new processes, tasks, and techniques.

While my present employment is satisfactory and productive, I am convinced that my potential is not being effectively utilized. I am seeking a responsible position that offers challenge and opportunity.

CRITICAL VIEWPOINT:

Chris's counselor devised a good strategy for him. The targeted format discourages the tendency to pigeonhole that is inherent in a more standard format. Chris's degree is listed at the bottom to minimize his lack of business education. His cover letter is upbeat, and one can sense in it his enthusiasm and his openness to learning.

CHRISTOPHER M. KOHL
8562 Lanhart Road
Little Rock, AR 72204
(501) 555-3941

JOB TARGET: MANAGEMENT TRAINEE–MATERIALS MANAGEMENT

CAPABILITIES

- Interview vendors to obtain product information, pricing and delivery date.
- Discuss defects of goods with quality control or inspection personnel to determine source of trouble and take corrective actions.
- Keep computerized records pertaining to inventory, costs, and deliveries.
- Make sound decisions based on personal experience and judgment as well as verifiable facts and data.
- Work long hours without physical stress or annoyance.

ACHIEVEMENTS

- Supervised and coordinated trucking terminal workers' activities and assignments in distribution and loading of goods.
- Inspected shipments for damage, and trained dock workers in correct ways to handle different kinds of material.
- Processed and handled billing documents.
- Handled customer complaints by determining freight location and estimating time of delivery using nationwide IBM communications system.
- Located and expedited rush shipments.

WORK HISTORY

Operations Coordinator
HOLLIS TRUCK LINES, INC.   Little Rock, AR   1992–present

Office Help/Laborer
WOODLEY CONSTRUCTION COMPANY   Little Rock, AR   1988–1992

EDUCATION

Bachelor of Science   Policy and Administration, University of Arkansas   1992

EMPLOYMENT SITUATION:

Joan was a former elementary school teacher who, after ten years at home raising children, was facing a divorce and re-entry into the world of the full-time job. In her ten years away from paid work she had accumulated volunteer experience and credits. She lacked a sense of her own worth outside of teaching, which she didn't want to do again. She targeted the field of health-care administration.

STRATEGIES FOR SUCCESS:

Joan's career counselor had Joan brainstorming pages of details about her achievements in teaching, homemaking, and her volunteer activities. Although sixty percent of what she wrote was not kept for the resume, expressing what she'd accomplished greatly enhanced Joan's self-esteem.

COVER LETTER STATEMENTS:

I understand your office is a beehive of activity, including long days of patient visits, filling out insurance forms, and balancing scheduled and emergency appointments.

I believe there are few medical office managers who combine office efficiency and effectiveness with maintaining caring patient relationships. I offer myself as an exception who can bring your administrative needs and patient communications to a very workable level.

CRITICAL VIEWPOINT:

Joan strengthened and internalized her ability to express her personal value after she completed her resume. She role-played interviews and telephone calls with three close friends as part of a full campaign on a well-researched list of potential employers.

(Second page covers work experience and nonpaid work experience in separate categories.)

JOAN KREBS
222 House Avenue
Sanatoga, PA 19464
(215) 555-6119

JOB OBJECTIVE:

Administrator—health care—utilizing skills in client/patient interaction, organization, and office management.

QUALIFICATIONS:

CLIENT/PATIENT INTERACTION

- Worked with senior citizens through the process of their relocation. Provided guidance and moral support to help clients feel relaxed about the move. Complimented for being empathic to clients' feelings and needs.
- Taught schoolchildren and developed their self-confidence through positive reinforcement of their achievements. Parents expressed improved self-images in their children at parent/teacher conferences.
- Motivated children to learn by showing enthusiasm for subjects being taught. Principals' observation reports acknowledged this enthusiasm as influencing children's desire for learning.
- Established an environment of warmth and self-control in the classroom. Increased academic productivity and cooperation.
- Worked with American Red Cross blood drives. Decreased donors' stress levels by showing compassion.

ORGANIZATION

- Led teams of packers in the operation of moving senior citizens. Kept clients' costs to a minimum by organizing and coordinating all project aspects.
- Developed and initiated a color coding system to expedite the unpacking and arrangement of clients' possessions in their new homes. Owner of the company noted the success of the system and adopted its usage throughout the organization.
- Organized and planned classroom activities. Principals and parents noted children's academic progress.
- Planned, scheduled and assigned volunteers for church service groups, improving overall efficiency.

OFFICE MANAGEMENT

- Maintained family budget for ten years. Reduced interest charges by recording expenses and keeping within allocated budget.
- Revised guidelines for the operation of church duties. Complimented for concise and well-thought-out instructions.

President—Women's Varsity Club—1971

EMPLOYMENT SITUATION:

For nine years Anna had managed a family-owned massage, nail, and beauty business that had grown and expanded tremendously. She was a significant factor in its huge success but she received little credit and a small salary. She felt that her three older brothers would eventually squeeze her out of the business. In spite of her family's disapproval, she decided to leave the family business to run a large cosmetic firm.

Anna traveled on her own to famous skin care houses and beauty salons to take courses and expand her knowledge base. Her resume had to portray her as an expert in the field with outstanding education, credentials, and experience.

This was Anna's first opportunity to shine as she branched out on her own in the world.

STRATEGIES FOR SUCCESS:

Anna's counselor helped her identify her daily duties and the skills it took to accomplish so many tasks. Anna practiced writing accomplishment statements to use in her resume and in the interviewing process. Her counselor identified power verbs that fit her situation and Anna used them throughout her resume and her cover letter.

COVER LETTER STATEMENTS:

My broad entrepreneurial experience, particularly in expanding our family business, could be very useful to you in the marketing and public relations arenas.

As cited on my resume, our salon was selected from among three hundred competitors to develop a hair-and-skin-care line. I have documentation and photographs in a small portfolio that I would be happy to show you.

CRITICAL VIEWPOINT:

This is an example of a case in which good career counseling is essential. Frequently people who inherit a position in a family business have no idea how they can translate their accomplishments into working for others. Confidence-building was essential here, and it was achieved.

ANNA LACEK
22 Breezy Point Harbor
Sarasota, FL 34236
(813) 555-0735

WORK EXPERIENCE:

1984-present   **LES TROIS CYPRES SPA**   Sarasota, FL
             Spa Manager

- Designed, implemented and directed a full service beauty spa.
- Escalated a two-room spa to one of national recognition and tripled business within seven years.
- Salon was selected from several hundred by a major corporation to develop a hair and skin care line.
- Prepared for national opening of two salons, visiting each personally to train staff and set up the entire operation.
- Consulted with advertising agencies to develop a contemporary concept of personalized skin care.
- Authored a full training manual encompassing all aspects of spa management and wrote a reference sequel for employees.
- Hosted several on-location Channel 8 TV interviews; quoted in national magazines for several photo shootings.
- Conducted highly successful seminar series for plastic surgeons and dermatologists. Spoke to groups from 50 to 1,500 with equal ease. Sought after as a speaker in the beauty care field.
- Researched expertise of beauty experts and hosted monthly meetings to continually upgrade staff and skills.

1983–1984   **GEORGETTE KLINGER, INC.**   Boca Raton, FL
           Makeup Artist

- Performed wide variety of functions including makeup sales of over $500 per day, and 20 to 30 make-up applications per 12-hour day.

EDUCATION:

1986   International Congress Symposium   Monte Carlo, France
            Certification in Training Techniques—Full Service Salons
1984   Dale Carnegie Course
            Certified for Effective Presentation
1981–1983   National Academy of Hairdressing
            Licensed Cosmetologist and Esthetician

EMPLOYMENT SITUATION:

Ginger was a recent college graduate with very strong background in sports, religious activities, and foreign languages. She wanted to teach high school Spanish and, if possible, coach sports as well.

STRATEGIES FOR SUCCESS:

Her resume needed to communicate her strong interpersonal and sports skills, volunteer activities, and primary career goal (teaching Spanish) in a way that was credible and appealing. This was a multitalented person presenting a dual focus.

Her career advisor had her put her master's degree at the top, followed by her undergraduate degrees in Spanish and psychology. She listed both career objectives right up front. A functional format grouped and focused her skills and experience. In her marketing letter she used quotes from others to spark interest.

COVER LETTER STATEMENTS:

I'm taking the liberty of quoting a few words from my supervisors, teachers and peers: 'Mature and sensitive beyond her age' . . . 'Poised and confident' . . . 'Creative . . . Optimistic . . . Determined . . . Outstanding motivator . . . Resourceful and innovative . . .'

I bring a unique blend of tenacity, humor, flexibility, leadership skills, and qualities that help youngsters enjoy learning. I am able to give you a lot of skill for your employer investment, as I function equally well as a Spanish teacher and sports coach; you can hire the abilities of two teachers in one.

CRITICAL VIEWPOINT:

Rarely do we suggest putting two career objectives up front on a resume. This case was an exception. Ginger's *primary* career objective is presented first, however, so that her dual focus does not confuse the reader.

She included an aggressive, businesslike approach in her self-marketing statements. As educators are having to think more and more in business terms, a direct economic appeal is smart thinking!

GINGER LA FARGE
117 Kingsbury Rd
Bridgeport, CT 06610
(203) 555-6756

EDUCATION:

University of Bridgeport	Bridgeport, CT	M. Education	1993
University of Connecticut	Storrs, CT	B.A. Psych/Spanish	1992

CAREER OBJECTIVE: To teach Spanish in a Grade 7-12 public school environment.

SECONDARY OBJECTIVE: To teach/coach after-school sports.

TEACHING EXPERIENCE:
- Substitute-taught in all academic areas.
- Taught tennis lessons to youths, adults.
- Volunteered with handicapped children / Children's Hospital.
- Organized children's activities; served as teacher's aide,
  Bridgeport, Connecticut summer school program.
- Led Catholic retreat weekend discussions with adults, teens.

SPANISH TRAINING/TEACHING:
- Taught Spanish on all ability levels.
- Tutored Bridgeport H.S. students in Spanish.
- Studied at University of Granada, Granada, Spain speaking
  only Spanish, living with local family.

SPORTS SKILLS/AWARDS/EXPERIENCE:
- Achieved #1 in both Singles/Doubles Varsity Tennis Team.
- Ranked #3 in Big East Tennis; #2 in state of Connecticut.
- High School: 1) elected Captain—varsity volleyball/tennis teams.
                2) named all-prep American athlete.
- Organized children's and adults' tennis program.

AFFILIATIONS:

1993–Present	Bridgeport Public Schools INTERN / ATHLETIC COACH	Bridgeport, CT
1988–Present	Lawndale Country Club HEAD TENNIS PRO / ASS'T TENNIS PRO	Bridgeport, CT
1983–1987	Bridgeport Town Recreation Program Bridgeport Summer School Program	Bridgeport, CT

EMPLOYMENT SITUATION:

Carolyn was a high-level education executive in the Midwest who wished to shift to the private sector in corporate training. She had a typical four-page rambling resume full of an educator's technical jargon that couldn't be read easily by any business executive.

STRATEGIES FOR SUCCESS:

Carolyn came into the market when training budgets were being trimmed nationwide and the market was bursting with people already experienced in the field. With the help of her counselor and her own research in the field, Carolyn pinpointed her interest in training and development for special-case employees. Where the usual corporate enhancement programs were being tabled during lean times, substance abuse was still a critical issue for human resource professionals. In some companies, developing talented people with learning disabilities was also gaining importance. This gave Carolyn a two-pronged approach. She wrote a functional resume stressing results.

COVER LETTER STATEMENTS:

As a seasoned education executive and former consultant, I can bring to your training department a unique ability to synthesize diverse programs and a sensitivity to special-case employees.

My professional affiliations with AMA and the Iowa Drug and Alcohol Dependency Council have educated me as to the corporate issues that currently affect human resources and general health within the corporate community. I'm thoroughly knowledgeable about state laws, as well as the relevant private and public programs.

With my specialty in the field of learning disabilities, I can introduce and implement entire programs to identify and develop talented employees who might be at risk within a particular work environment.

CRITICAL VIEWPOINT:

Carolyn trimmed the heavy jargon from her resume and used everyday language. She spent almost six months researching her new field while she was still safe and comfortable in her current job.

(Second page covers work history, education, and professional affiliations.)

CAROLYN LANDERS
7523 Sutton Place
Des Moines, IA 50322
(515) 555-7852 (Home)
(515) 555-2413 (Office)

MANAGEMENT / ADMINISTRATION :
Designed and implemented highly innovative educational programs in
diverse areas.

ACHIEVEMENTS

- Initiated practices to successfully recruit/develop key personnel who were
  promoted into top positions.
- Served as first woman consultant in Iowa as an expert in Pupil
  Personnel/Special Services; advised on issues to the Governor and
  Legislative branches.
- Managed several system-wide budgets totaling $16M; ensured creativity
  while adhering to constraints.
- Coordinated transportation program for handicapped persons from county-
  wide area.
- Planned and implemented dynamic staff development programs that
  became focal point for creative thinking and state model for 169 towns.
- Wrote and monitored state and federal grant proposals; successfully won
  over $1M.
- Facilitated highly successful District Mentor Program.
- Set local policy for monitoring of individual educational plans.
- Designed district group testing program in compliance with state
  requirements; monitored results and initiated competency requirements to
  ensure development.
- Developed exemplary early childhood model programs for children at risk
  and severely retarded children.
- Established highly innovative parent education programs resulting in
  significantly enhancing community/school relationships.

COMMUNICATION / TRAINING :
Served as Regional Director of teacher practicums, with 15 years in
research of learning dysfunctions.

- Served as primary advocate for learning-disabled while publicly supporting
  efforts of educators, parents, and administrators.
- Conducted highly respected in-service programming on a local, state and
  regional basis.
- Trained and taught on both the undergradute and graduate levels in areas
  of speech, reading, program development and supervision.
- Sought-after speaker on the professional and university levels in areas of
  educating handicapped populations and related legal issues.

PR

198

198

196

ED

PR

-
- I
- E
- Who's Who in American Education, selected 1991–92

EMPLOYMENT SITUATION:

Jeffrey was in the process of a career move within his own large corporation. Due to his technical knowledge and excellent customer contact capabilities, he had been temporarily promoted to training customer service representatives. With a sudden hiring freeze and a subsequent drop in training requirements, he was returned to his original job and out of management. Now that he had a six-month taste of training and management, however, this became his long-term goal.

STRATEGIES FOR SUCCESS:

Jeffrey had no bachelor's degree, no management experience, and only six months in an official training position. The competition of many managers competing for a few training jobs was strong. His counselor selected the functional resume format for him so he could list Training first, then add Public Contact and Sales.

He was encouraged to take up public speaking in his community and volunteer as a trainer for the Red Cross to expand his resume value statements.

COVER LETTER STATEMENTS:

I am sending you my resume in response to a job opening listed for the Training Sales Manager position in Phoenix. I have been very involved in training course development and delivery in the past year. One of the two-day courses that I designed, developed, and facilitated was integrated into a larger project in government and education services.

My extensive experience in the design and implementation of sales campaigns for outlying offices may also prove helpful when delivering training to remote locations becomes a necessity during times of budget restriction.

CRITICAL VIEWPOINT:

Jeffrey was compelled to network heavily as this was a very highly competitive time in his company. He quickly went through dozens of calls, singling out four or five professional contacts who could initiate interviews for him within his company.

(Second page covers his work history and education. Because this was an internal resume, Jeffrey was allowed to keep the excessive internal references. This language would be made generic if he were leaving the company.)

JEFFREY LANE
720 Field Ways
Denver, CO 80226
(303) 555-7379 (h)
(303) 555-6504 (w)

TRAINING/INSTRUCTION

- Developed and presented detailed training material relating to specific products and service for Home and Personal Services market units and the Central Dispatch Administration Center.
- Conducted instructor-led 12-week Accelerated Learning Service Representative Training for new hires and intracompany transfers.
- Taught usage, and demonstrated skills and techniques which improved expertise of Home and Personal Service Technicians, Maintenance Administrators, and Order Writers in technical and customer service functions on the Centron product line.
- Delivered regional deregulated billing methods training and received outstanding commendations.
- Prepared appraisals and conducted biweekly reviews of performance and productivity.
- Identified barriers to satisfactory performance and developed action plans for improvement.
- Coached, motivated and encouraged open participation to develop group dynamics and cohesiveness among students to accelerate learning during on-job and classroom instruction.
- Facilitated workshops with Home and Personal Services service representatives to increase awareness, develop and improve selling skills and techniques.

PUBLIC CONTACT

- Resolved customer and corporation commission complaints, billing and toll claims, and negotiated payment arrangements for customers throughout Metro Phoenix, Northern Arizona, and Colorado.
- Negotiated complex exchange service orders and repair requests for residence and business customers, and insured timely completion.
- Managed installation of customer services by coordinating among customers, engineering, construction, network, dispatch and business office functions.
- Represented Western Allied community referral service to provide information to help citizens experiencing life crises.
- Elected to the community planning committee of the Board of Directors at Professional Community Management Association to plan, implement and oversee environmental changes.

SALES

- Received merit award in the "Winners Circle" for consistently achieving outstanding sales.
- Designed and implemented office promotions, campaigns, sales contests and kick-offs designed to stimulate market penetration of enhanced ESS and basic exchange services.
- Operated numerous computer systems and input precise data insuring completion of sales and service orders processed through assignment, network, load control, dispatch, and installation departments.
- Served as Subject Matter Expert on Centron products and motivated others to increase sales.
- Reviewed individual monthly sales reports, maintained sales objectives, identified areas of improvement, realigned goals and implemented corrective action to improve performance.
- Designed customized packages for business and residence customers which increased revenue 9%.

WESTERN TELECOMMUNICATIONS TECHNICAL, SALES, MOTIVATIONAL, INSTRUCTOR
AND MANAGEMENT TRAINING, Phoenix, Arizona, and Denver, Colorado

EMPLOYMENT SITUATION:

At fifty-two, Carl accepted early retirement after twenty-six years with one major retail organization. He survived well enough for two years doing piecework and consulting assignments, but finally missed the income and benefits of working steadily for one organization. He had multiple skills, but had trouble deciding which area of business he wanted to pursue.

STRATEGIES FOR SUCCESS:

Carl's career counselor reduced his resume from four pages to two. Carl was encouraged to seek employment in smaller companies that would appreciate his expertise. He wanted a $100-million or smaller company, which, although not small, was still a considerable change from his previous employer.

COVER LETTER STATEMENT:

My more than twenty-five years of retail merchandising for consumers' products demonstrates my ability to:

- manage sales organizations

- develop and implement advertising/promotional materials

- budget and achieve targeted profit levels

- communicate, both orally and in written form, to all levels of the organization

- analyze markets to achieve increased sales and market penetration

Your company has an excellent reputation in the retail industry. I feel that my experience would allow me to make an immediate contribution to the company, and I would like to discuss how this experience might be put to work for you now or in the future.

CRITICAL VIEWPOINT:

Carl wrote a good results-oriented functional resume; however, he could have made reference to a specific industry in his objective. Seeking counseling and reducing the resume from four pages to two helped him generate interviews he wouldn't have obtained otherwise.

(Second page covers employment history, education, and supporting data.)

CARL P. LANSING
75 Longfellow Road
Cambridge, MA 02138
(617) 555-8559

OBJECTIVE:

- General Management in a multi-unit sales-oriented retail/distribution organization up to $500 million.

ACCOMPLISHMENTS:

I. GENERAL MANAGEMENT of multi-units with sales in excess of $75 million, responsible for:

- Establishing and approving sales and operating budgets.
- Creating and implementing sales, merchandising, advertising and promotional strategies.
- Directing and staffing organizational structure.
- Analyzing market data to determine store locations and negotiate leases.
- Developing 12 new licensed businesses which contributed over $900,000 profit annually.

II. MERCHANDISE MANAGEMENT

- Reduced electrical divisions' stock-keeping units by 20%. Results improved sales by 9% and gross profit by 1.1% through planogram revisions and investing in inventory depth.
- Initiated a multifaceted marketing program to improve market penetration for detergent. Effort culminated in 10 stores selling over one million pounds of detergent in a 30-day period.
- Coordinated menu planning/product buying plan for the restaurant division which improved profit contribution from 5% to 11%.

III. SALES MANAGEMENT

- Managed inside, outside, and telemarketing organizations of up to 600 people.
- Structured and administered a pay-for-performance program for over 400 people, improving morale and performance.
- Developed a point-of-sale presentation and training package that resulted in increased average transaction value.
- Established a cross-selling plan which improved seasonal sales by 100% over two years.

- Merchant Goal Achievement—three years
- Boston Chamber of Commerce—Membership committee

EMPLOYMENT SITUATION:

When Judith was still a college student, she met a top-notch career counselor who helped her put her first resume together. At the time she wanted to gather some really good business credits with high-quality companies. A real go-getter, she worked for two big companies and achieved extraordinary success in her first three years out of school. Inspired by her counselor's resume work, Judith did free-lance resume-writing for recent college graduates during her after-work hours.

STRATEGIES FOR SUCCESS:

After two years and scores of happy customers, Judith decided to consider career counseling as a field. She resigned from her full-time position and after an apprentice period with her college counselor, she hung out her shingle for business. Drawing largely on her successful reputation with past free-lance clients, she sent out a promotional brochure.

COVER LETTER STATEMENT:

[This is a sample list of accomplishments from the centerfold of her brochure:]

- Successfully completed resumes and marketing strategies in the fields of finance, engineering, human resources, the fine arts, sales, and marketing.

- Strategized job-finding techniques to empower individuals in a personalized and organized job campaign.

- Member of American Society of Training and Development.

- As sales representative with a major food manufacturing concern, I was given a Salesperson of the Quarter award over twenty-six competitors.

Let me give you the insight and enthusiasm to market yourself for the career you want. I have acquired an excellent business record in a very short time, and have interpersonal and writing skills I can easily pass on to you.

CRITICAL VIEWPOINT:

The following is Judith's earlier salesperson resume, included here as an example of her work. Out of college only two years, she had successfully written an impressive chronological resume.

She completed the career change as soon as she felt she had gained enough confidence and practical experience in business, and in helping others with resumes and job campaigns.

Judith Mary Latham
735 Walser Road
Louisville, KY 40207
(502) 555-8302

EXPERIENCE:

1992-Present **Sales Representative   The Silverton Company**   Louisville, KY
- Establish print advertising in account locations to generate consumer trial and usage.
- Prepare and deliver presentations to increase sales, distribution, and consumer impact.
- Independently manage personal field office. Accountabilities include time management and efficiently coordinating administrative services from local vendors.
- Serve as one point of contact to all Silverton grocers, wholesalers, and end users for over 100 products in each account.
- Awarded Salesperson of the Quarter, from 27 salespeople, after first full quarter with company.
- Won national second prize in Fall 1992 Creative Display Contest.

1991-1992 **Sales Service Coordinator   Electro-Globe**   Louisville, KY
- Attended training program hosted by two shut-down facilities of corporate consolidation.
- Managed eight large O.E.M. sales accounts.
- Dramatically reduced customer billing claims through innovative group process intervention.
- Answered 50-100 calls per day interfacing with customers, sales, marketing, and manufacturing.

1990-1991 **Intern   Kentucky Power and Light Company**   Lexington, KY
- Received one of two internship programs offered.
- Administered and facilitated stand-up classroom training.
- Developed permanent course material on motivation for Fundamentals of Effective Supervision course.
- Developed and statistically analyzed course evaluations for Total Quality and Management Development Classes.
- Developed draft of company's first-ever comprehensive training needs analysis to assess training needs of over 8,000 employees.

1989-1991 **Sales Associate   The Railroad Shop**   Lexington, KY
- Worked as second job to help pay for college.
- Consistently led sales force in sale dollars per purchase, sales per hour and items per purchase.

EDUCATION:

University of Kentucky, Lexington, KY
Graduated June 1991, G.P.A. in major 3.6/4.0
Bachelor of Arts—Human Resource Development

CIVIC/PROFESSIONAL:

- American Management Association, member
- American Society for Training and Development, national and local member
- National Association for Female Executives, professional member
- Center for the Study of the Presidency, invited to attend 1991 conference "The U.S. and the Pacific Rim," member
- Literacy Volunteers of America, certified active tutor

EMPLOYMENT SITUATION:

Robin had a very diverse background as a high school language teacher, then a college instructor, and finally in a recent series of jobs in TV, advertising and promotion. She had also run a small diving equipment shop for three years. She wanted now to refocus her career into teaching communications in a university.

STRATEGIES FOR SUCCESS:

Robin not only had many careers, but had also lived all over the U.S. and Europe. There were numerous gaps in her work history due to frequent moves (her husband was in the military) and child-rearing. Robin's career advisor suggested a two-page functional resume. To ease the task of pulling a common thread through all the other jobs, she omitted the details of the diving equipment shop experience.

COVER LETTER STATEMENTS:

I am a professional educator/media communicator with twenty years of results-oriented experience in television, public schools, corporations, and higher education.

I have been acknowledged for outstanding skill teaching all ages and learning styles. I have been an instructor of French, English, and communications. While living in France I also served as a tour guide for all nationalities. I have designed multi media productions for advertising, and served as a TV talk-show hostess, conducting timely and complex interviews in front of live audiences.

CRITICAL VIEWPOINTS:

Robin's resume pulls together a multitude of unrelated jobs. One should not fault Robin for her varied jobs; she had the talent and energy to earn her way in circumstances that demanded she be flexible. She had multiple talents, and she used them.

(Second page covers six of the jobs she held over twenty years, and education.)

ROBIN LEAHY
410 Biltmore Way
Miami, Florida 33134
(305) 555-8593

COMMUNICATIONS:

Wrote TV commercials and slide presentations for health care professionals, serving as Public Information Officer for the Appalachian Regulatory Commission. Hosted and produced over 75 public affairs TV broadcasts in Kentucky and captivated thousands of tourists as a bilingual tour guide in Western France.

Created an innovative approach to marketing real estate by using home videos computerized for showing in the comfort of the real estate office. This effort has resulted in the concept still being used in five Miami area firms.

BROADCAST JOURNALISM / PROGRAM HOST:

Broadcasted news to the visually impaired of Dade and Broward counties in Florida; Hosted MedAlert programs on television featuring discussions with medical professionals; coordinated all research, remote taping, on-the-air interviews and follow-up with the public.

Designed and created customer relations programs and training for video industry. Wrote video vignettes, casted, scheduled and completed several program series. Worked directly with Floor Director, Technical Director. Prepared sets, acted, and directed final edit.

INSTRUCTION / TRAINING:

Taught conversational French. Created innovative audio-language curriculum resulting in students speaking by third lesson. Taught English as well as "English as a Second Language" in Western France.

Taught junior and senior high school grammar and literature and all levels of French. Established diverse learning-modality teaching programs to capture attention and hold interest. Taught same methodology on the college level with undergraduates, as well as adults in the School of Continuing Education.

New Paltz, NY   B.A. Cum Laude

EMPLOYMENT SITUATION:

At fifty-five Harold had been recently laid off and was in the midst of divorce proceedings. He felt he was "over the hill." His internal conflicts interfered with his phone techniques and face-to-face interviews. Devastated by his lay-off, he no longer felt important enough to obtain a regular position. Although he was working with a psychotherapist, he was not yet ready to sell himself aggressively.

STRATEGIES FOR SUCCESS:

Harold and his career counselor devised an interim plan for Harold to hire himself out through a "temp" agency to build up his self-esteem. Part-time work was challenging to his talents and kept some money flowing in. There were a number of professional temp agencies that could place Harold easily once he was willing to accept that workstyle.

COVER LETTER STATEMENTS:

I have decided to break away from full-time employment for a brief period and take on short assignments. I believe any organization would be invigorated by having a skilled generalist like myself solving their problems.

I am equally capable in applied research, advanced development, and prototype design in systems or applications software, applying and expanding theoretical and mathematical aspects as needed.

My particular interests include parallel and data flow processing, programming languages, and programs or systems that interact strongly with operating systems, especially UNIX.

CRITICAL VIEWPOINT:

Harold's story is very typical of the workplace since the early 1980s. Many white-collar wage earners in their early or middle fifties have been suddenly laid off and left wondering what to do next. In Harold's case, his supervisor at his first temp position was so pleased with his work that he was asked to stay on permanently. This bolstered his self-esteem, and he accepted the offer. The counselor's strategy had been wise: Harold had needed to take action to revive his energy and keep the money coming in.

(Second page covers work history and education.)

HAROLD G. LOGAN, Ph.D.
52 Horse Hill Road
Hanover, NH 03750
(603) 555-0837

TECHNICAL STRENGTHS:

Generalist, integrating knowledge from diverse specialty areas.
Experienced in designing, coding, and enhancing language processors and
system software tools.
Skilled in mathematical and numerical analysis and algorithm development.
Broadly familiar with electronics, computer hardware, and interfacing.

EMPLOYMENT HISTORY:

1991 to present: **SYMTEX CORPORATION**   Boxford, MA
 Principal Software Engineer—Designed, coded, and tested
 menu-driven diagnostic tools for a REGULUS-based embedded system;
 specified, implemented, and tested REGULUS and ROM support of a
 SCSI disk; investigated redesign of interprocessor communications
 and preliminary design of a command file interpreter.

Spring & Fall 1990 (part-time): **BOSTON UNIVERSITY**   Boston, MA
 Instructor—taught UNIX system programming and internals in
 state-of-the-art courses.

1988 to 1991: **MAGNUM ELECTRONICS**   Boston, MA
 Senior Software Engineer—developed and tested various
 UNIX-resident communications programs; conceived, developed, and
 tested a high-level language and a supporting preprocessor for a data
 flow graphics device; ported a C compiler and two assemblers to the
 Intel MDS development system.

1987 to 1988: **DESIGN AND CREATIVE SCIENCES INC.**   Boxford, MA
 Communications Engineer on contract to MIT Lincoln Laboratories.
 Enhanced a head of a gateway in an experimental voice-carrying
 packet-switched network; added modem control capabilities to a UNIX
 tty driver.

1986 to 1987 (part-time): **SELF-EMPLOYED**   Boston, MA
 On contract to Century Computer Systems, Westfield, MA—designed
 efficient FFT algorithms, free of bit reversal, and coded them for a
 pipelined array processor.

Massachusetts Institute of Technology
 • B.A., Physics, High Honors

EMPLOYMENT SITUATION:

Virginia had a satisfying job and felt no reason to leave it, except for her feeling that she was underpaid. She decided to seek a substantial raise consistent with her contribution to the company's excellent public image. As she was newly married and establishing a home, she wanted only to increase her income without making a serious move.

STRATEGY FOR SUCCESS:

Virginia used career counseling to increase her assertiveness. She knew she had her nose so deeply in her job that she had little time to promote the value she brought to the company. Her counselor convinced her to write a resume that could also be used externally, in case the internal strategy failed. She had Virginia list fifty statements about her everyday tasks at work, using precise numbers and self-acknowledging objectives. As she compiled this list and wrote her resume, her self-esteem grew.

COVER LETTER STATEMENTS:

[This is an internal memo to her manager.]

Based on my accomplishments and potential, I'm interested in expanding my work and my salary within the company. I've just completed a resume I thought you should see. This is an important growth period for me. Can we have lunch or coffee later this week? I'd like to share with you my ideas for the next steps in my career within our great company.

CRITICAL VIEWPOINT:

Virginia's resume has more flag-waving for her company than is usually included. As it was purposely designed for an internal promotion, she gave it her public relations flair, crediting the company as well as herself. She came out of her shell, and she sought and received a 20 percent raise.

VIRGINIA MADDAN
769 Huntly Road
Charlotte, NC 28227
704-555-4831 Home
704- 555-6256 Office

QUALIFICATIONS SUMMARY:
Created and produced *HARTON* magazine, the widely recognized shipping and distribution magazine of the Hart-Compton Group. With a circulation of 18,000, this highly respected publication is frequently quoted in the trade press.

Developed and managed Office of Immigration Affairs for the Hart-Compton Group. Established reputation as expert in matters of immigration law and procedure.

1980–Present
HART-COMPTON INC.   Charlotte, NC
The industry leader in worldwide ocean transportation and specialty storage.

EDITOR, *HARTON* MAGAZINE
• Create and produce corporate magazine for worldwide distribution.
• Establish content, format, and style.
• Direct the activities of writers, typesetters, graphic designers, photographers, and printers.
• Set editorial policy and objectives with senior management; report directly to Chairman and Chief Executive Officer.

1985–Present
PUBLIC RELATIONS
• Establish and administer corporate graphic standards, defining the visual style for all company communications and strengthening its public image.
• Produce advertisements, capabilities brochures, promotional materials, departmental manuals, special projects.
• Write and publish the President's Update, a biweekly newsletter from the president to all employees.
• Write, proofread, and copy-edit presentations made by senior management.

1980–1985
MANAGER, U.S. IMMIGRATION
• Manage a complete immigration service for international employees relocating to and from the U.S., keeping fully current with prevailing laws, regulations, local practices and conditions.
• Recommend to top management appropriate options for recruitment and relocation of personnel depending upon visa status.
• Maintain liaison relationship with government and legal authorities; coordinate with in-house and outside counsel.
• Prepare petitions, applications, motions to the Departments of Justice, State, and Labor.
• Save company up to $150,000 per year in legal fees.

1975–1980
U.S. HOUSE OF REPRESENTATIVES   Washington, DC
LEGISLATIVE ASSISTANT
• Researched legislation, prepared correspondence for signature, worked with committee staff in preparation for hearings, conducted casework through various agencies.
• Designed, wrote, and circulated congressman's quarterly newsletter to constituents.

EDUCATION:
UNIVERSITY OF NORTH CAROLINA, Chapel Hill   B.A. Eng/Psych
Phi Beta Kappa   Psi Chi Honorary Society

EMPLOYMENT SITUATION:

After a steady thirty-year work history in electronics and computer design, Jay was laid off during a slow period. Due to a recession, there was little hope of his being hired full-time in his technical specialty. Jay was discouraged and pessimistic.

STRATEGIES FOR SUCCESS:

Jay's career advisor set out to rebuild his confidence. With a little prodding, Jay volunteered to chair his professional association's lecture committee. Meeting prestigious people in his field on a social level bolstered his self-esteem, which enabled Jay to work next at collecting evidence that he was not considered a has-been by his professional colleagues. At his counselor's suggestion he requested from his last boss a reference that went beyond his technical skills. He got the reference and warm words of praise. His change in career direction was geared to the stressful conditions in the work environment.

COVER LETTER STATEMENTS:

At the suggestion of my colleague Ed Hollander, I'm initiating this contact with the idea of arranging an informal conversation with you about how to deal with the high stress your division has been facing with your recent budget cuts and lay-offs. My former supervisor said he'd want me along on the 'last boat out in the choppy Red China Sea,' to help navigate people to sanity and safety. I've attached a copy of his reference letter. Perhaps I can help build morale in your group's pressured circumstances, and be part of your turnaround team.

CRITICAL VIEWPOINT:

Jay's volunteer work helped rebuild his confidence. His cover letter reflects a casual yet assertive quality that worked well for him. Within less than ninety days, he landed a consulting position with a prestigious Boston hospital that needed a morale boost.

JASPER L. MANNESE
819 Walden Road
Boston, MA 02119
(617) 555-9752

OBJECTIVE : PRINTED CIRCUIT DESIGNER/CHECKER, using technical, management, and human relations skills.

BACKGROUND : Extensive technical experience as follows:

- Printed circuit design and optimization
- Final schematic preparation
- Parts list derivation and generation
- Reviewing engineer input

- Board assembly and schematic checking
- Printed circuit artwork taping
- Relay logic and testing
- Cable design and fabrication

RELEVANT ACCOMPLISHMENTS :

Optimized circuit board designs by making modifications that increased reliability, manufacturability, heat transfer, noise reduction, and minimized signal paths.

Increased the ease of servicing P.C. boards by critiquing succeeding engineering schematic until prototypes and schematics were ready for release to manufacturing as an entity.

Generated unique library figures for different components using a CAD system in a data base, resulting in P.C. boards designed in a sophisticated but timely manner.

Designed and built van modifications to store luggage and allow sleeping space on long trips. Solution was a long raised rear deck that could be disassembled easily.

Collaborated in daily team meetings to design pellet boards and assemblies for Columbia IV. Team assignments included: deciding on schedules, revising plans as needed, and problem-solving.

EXPERIENCE :

- OPTICON **Senior P.C. Designer and Graphics Design Specialist**
  Boston, MA   1986–1992
- SOUTHBORO CORPORATION **P.C. Designer**
  Boston, MA   1977–1986
- FEATHERSTONE COMPUTER CONTROL
  Senior P.C. Designer in Modular Products Engineering Department
  Boston, MA   1968–1977
- FEATHERSTONE, EDP Division
  Design Draftsman, Checker, Layout Draftsman, Electronic Technician
  Boston, MA   1962–1968

EDUCATION :

Related Workshops: Basic Users Course for Opticon 870; Structural Analysis; Logic Design of Switching Circuits; FORTRAN IV; Digital Logic; AOS

Associate Degree Electronic Engineering, BOSTON COLLEGE.
Graduated MASSACHUSETTS RADIO AND TELEVISION SCHOOL.

EMPLOYMENT SITUATION:

Holly had an excellent educational background and kept current in her field—geriatric counseling—through her private clients, reading, and listening to tape-recorded case studies. She wanted to work in the public sector as a counselor for special-needs adults.

Holly was blind, but had a fairly good employment history working with sighted as well as visually handicapped people. She wanted to play down her blindness, but not exclude it from her resume. She also had "breaks" in her employment record due to several illnesses that had kept her out of work as much as a year at a time.

STRATEGIES FOR SUCCESS:

Holly's career counselor suggested the functional format to downplay the spotty employment record and highlight her accomplishments with the focus on community service. Her handicap was mentioned subtly in a single sentence: "Travel independently with a guide dog."

COVER LETTER STATEMENTS:

I understand you will be opening a new eldercare facility in northern Dutchess County in ninety days, and you're seeking an experienced residential staff.

I have an extensive practical background in working with the elderly, in both private practice and clinical settings. I am also able to assume a residential position. I offer not only understanding, but direct knowledge and experience of living a full life even with a disability.

CRITICAL VIEWPOINT:

Holly never said in her letter or resume that she was blind, but the message was clear. She was hired as a nursing home family counselor within forty-five days of starting her job campaign.

HOLLY LAKER MANTIS
160 Lower Lake Road
Hartford, CT 06467
(203) 555-1496

MANAGEMENT / COMMUNITY SERVICE :

Located suitable housing and employment for retarded and handicapped individuals. Networked extensively in community with employers. Referred clients to specialized skill classes to upgrade daily functioning. Created small group homes in the community where five or six handicapped people could live independently. Investigated communities where group homes could be developed, and identified municipal services available, with special attention to convenience, recreational facilities, shopping, and hospitals. Played an instrumental role in educating public to accept group homes.

COUNSELING / INSTRUCTION :

Counseled individuals in one-on-one and group settings. Assessed cases to determine appropriate placement. Evaluated clients regarding individual capabilities, housing needs and general living patterns. Established a workable program with clients. Advised individuals regarding their entitled benefits, referring them to direct sources of service. Provided follow-up services to outreach workers.

Taught braille to elderly convalescent home patients. Counseled elderly individuals with personal problems and assisted in grooming the aged.

Certified in CPR and participate as active member of Gerontology Society, National Rehabilitation Association, and American Council of the Blind.

Travel independently with a guide dog.

WORK HISTORY:

1986–Present	Self-employed private practice Specializing in individual therapy and hypnosis.	Hartford,CT
1984–85	CENTER FOR INDEPENDENT LIVING **Case Manager/Counselor**	Westport,CT
1982–83	CT ASSOCIATION OF RETARDED CITIZENS **Research Survey Worker**	Bridgeport, CT
1980–81	BRIDGEPORT CONVALESCENT CENTER **Internship—Gerontology**	Bridgeport,CT

EDUCATION:

1981	FAIRFIELD UNIVERSITY M.S. Counseling Concentration Gerontology	Fairfield, CT

PROFESSIONAL DEVELOPMENT:

1986–87	Certification, hypnotherapy In cooperation with Dr. Phillip Hanes	New Haven, CT
1986	Exceptional Cancer Patient Group Six-month internship with Dr. Bernard Siegel	Greenwich, CT

EMPLOYMENT SITUATION:

Christine was in the middle of a personal crisis. Her husband was terminally ill, and although she'd been away from the work world for several years, she was preparing to be self-supporting. Her background was in theater, education, and restaurant management. She'd also spent four years managing the theater careers of two child actors traveling throughout the United States and Europe. Christine had no clue as to career direction.

STRATEGIES FOR SUCCESS:

Her first draft of her resume was three pages long and rambling. She insisted on a resume that would summarize all her accomplishments as she launched a nondirected job search. Her counselor helped her pare the resume down to one page. She coached Christine to begin the campaign with local hotel chains where she could be in contact with the public.

COVER LETTER STATEMENTS:

As a teacher, I mastered skills in communication, creative flexibility, and adapting easily to new environments. I have trained mainly in hospitality and have drawn upon a wide variety of skills as a food services manager. I am comfortable with hard work and dealing with the public, and I handle change and conflict easily.

Over the years, I have developed the expertise and personality to offer substantial contributions in public relations, community events, dealing with corporate clientele, and planning events and affairs.

CRITICAL VIEWPOINT:

Many people who have outgoing personalities and a good head for detail select the travel, hotel, or food industries which offer a large variety of opportunities and flexible work hours. Christine's meandering work history would not be a hindrance as long as she came on strong in her interviews.

CHRISTINE MANUEL
442 Ardsley Place
Birmingham, AL 35209
(203) 335-2125

RESTAURANT MANAGEMENT :

- Established total front house system of a 300-seat business. Directed all hiring, training, motivating, and scheduling of 15-person staff. Handled payroll. Managed liquor and food orders and all inventory control.

- Interfaced with corporate clientele, successfully building strong relationships and repeat business. Directed unique set-up of three kitchens, with three separate sets of chefs. Became restaurant's first female manager and handled all operations with equal ease.

INSTRUCTION / TEACHING :

- Established art program, designing progressive curriculum for grades 1–8. Successfully taught youngsters of all abilities.

- Taught English and speech, and managed drama program for several hundred students. Designed and implemented a highly successful dropout prevention program for underprivileged students resulting in a dramatic shift in self-esteem, retention in school, and eventual decision to enter careers with a future.

THEATRICAL MANAGEMENT :

- Managed the professional careers of two children which included TV, commercials, movies, and Broadway. 1985-1988

- Assisted in children's productions with the Capron Studios, a Children's Theatre Workshop; handled coaching, staging and costuming. 1983–1986

EXPERIENCE :

1990-1993	Houlihan's Restaurant & Pub GENERAL MANAGER	Birmingham, AL
1989-1990	Yamiyuri Japanese Restaurant DAY MANAGER	Birmingham, AL
1980-1986	St. Sebastian School TEACHER	Montgomery, AL
1971-1974	Lincoln Middle School TEACHER	Montgomery, AL

EDUCATION :	UNIVERSITY OF ALABAMA SANFORD COLLEGE	One course to Master's Degree B.A.—English/Art

EMPLOYMENT SITUATION:

June worked ten years in one company. Her boss offered her various jobs up the ladder which she found unappealing because she would be required to relocate to achieve any growth. She had no college degree, and no idea what she wanted to do next.

STRATEGIES FOR SUCCESS:

Even though June was already thirty, she had never really competed in the job market before. Her career advisor taught her the structure of a good job campaign: focus on a job target or career objective; research through reading and personal contacts; write a resume; formulate self-marketing strategies; contact potential employers; and keep going until you're offered the right job.

June wanted a chronological resume because it showed off her growth and accomplishments. She targeted property management as a way to test the market and start her campaign. As she was uncertain of her final job target, she was unwilling to focus her resume other than chronologically.

COVER LETTER STATEMENTS:

You can see from my resume that I have a clear track record of steady growth in my company. I was awarded Manager of the Year two years in a row. I am able to handle all aspects of theater property management, from cost control to sensitive personnel issues. I'm seeking an opportunity to translate these talents and achievements to your industry.

CRITICAL VIEWPOINT:

Although June's counselor did a great job helping her to prepare a resume, June would have stood a better chance against the competition with a functional or targeted resume, guiding the potential employer to read her accomplishments through the lens of property management. This resume, however, does adequately describe her outstanding capabilities.

JUNE McDONALD
852 Shoreline Terrace
San Diego, CA 92021
(619) 555-4643

EMPLOYMENT HISTORY:

July 1983–present   **District Manager**
GLOBAL THEATRE CORP., San Diego, CA

Ten years of progressive accomplishments in theater management.

RESPONSIBILITIES:

• Manage general operations of 18 theaters and 90 screens in California, Arizona and Texas.
• Responsibility for corporate concerns, interests, and protection of company assets.
• Market Global Theatre Corp. with the goal of domination of the marketplace.
• Recruit, hire and train theater managers; develop human resources.
• Handle union and nonunion employee relations.
• Oversee theaters' safety practices and risk management.

ACHIEVEMENTS:

• Received seven promotions in as many years, far superseding the norm. With each promotion, took over troubled sites. In each instance, improved the situation significantly within 90 days.
• Streamlined expenses; reduced payroll and supply costs by up to 30%.
• Beat the corporate goal by achieving one of the lowest ratios of payroll to total overhead. Was one of two managers out of 11 who successfully met this goal. Awarded a twelve-day trip to Tahiti for the accomplishment.
• Significantly streamlined costs from FY 1992 to FY 1993; reduced supply costs by 20 percent and repair costs by 45 percent.
• Designed, developed, and managed an employee-training videotape program; allotted a $350,000 budget to work with a production company.
• Created and implemented a management training program which significantly improved the quality of management staff.
• Recognized as a corporate resource for handling sensitive personnel problems. Developed a reputation for achieving excellence in housekeeping and maintenance standards which are critical for providing quality customer service.
• Improved morale by being a highly visible manager and organizing corporate events, e.g. initiating district picnics.
• Recognized as company "Manager of the Year" during 1992 and 1993.
• Received assorted showmanship and marketing awards.

EDUCATION:

120 hours; Major—Psychology
University of Kansas, Kansas City

EMPLOYMENT SITUATION:

Sandy's primary concern was to find a work situation compatible with his value system. His current company just didn't support his personal management philosophy. An enthusiastic proponent of worker empowerment, he was seeking a situation that supported his ideas. He was ready to accept a lower salary and less responsibility in exchange for the proper environment. As he was committed to his community, he was unwilling to relocate.

STRATEGIES FOR SUCCESS:

Sandy sought to identify and access leaders who embraced the same human resource philosophy as his. Product, industry, and the size of the organization were of secondary concern. His career advisor suggested he include his philosophy in his cover letter, and his letters were therefore more philosophical than those of most senior managers. [However, almost all of his contacts were made in face-to-face meetings, rather than by mail.]

COVER LETTER STATEMENTS:

My philosophy is that in any job there are successes and learning experiences——never failures. I always encourage people to try to improve on the performance of their jobs by continually striving for enhanced results. I believe that the person who tries to jump over the moon may not make it, but he will certainly go higher than the person who tries to jump over the fence. I practice management by objectives, and believe that an organization's goals and objectives must be known and understood at all levels.

When I spoke about my approach in a conversation with Harvey Olenstein, he identified you as someone sharing the same views, someone who "walks what he talks."

CRITICAL VIEWPOINT:

Sandy's approach is inspirational. He has made it to the "top" in business as a senior-level manager with a successful corporation. He is personally committed to an environment that fosters personal development, and his cover letter is direct and eloquent about his needs and his desire to fulfill them.

(Second page covers his early career, his community activities and education.)

SANFORD T. McGRORY
22 Cachepit Way
Cincinnati, OH 45227
(513) 555-7986 Office
(513) 555-9941 Home

OBJECTIVE: Senior-level management in a community-involved, people-oriented
             environment.

1984 –Present   THE STANDARD FOOD COMPANY

PLANT MANAGER, Cincinnati Food Processing   1991–Present
Responsible for overall operation of a $30-60M FDA/USDA food processing
plant, including cost center control, manufacturing, distribution, and human
resource development. Reported to the Vice-President of Operations. Plant
employed up to 400 operations employees with a staff ranging from 25 to 80
managers and professionals. Products produced included Orangeade and full
line of San Giorgio products. Promoted to return plant to cost-effective
operation and improve development of human resources.

Major Accomplishments: Improved productivity in San Giorgio by 25% over
2+ years and in Orangeade by over 45% in 3 years. Revitalized cost reduction
program such that results exceeded $6.0 million over 2 years. Improved labor
relations climate in plant, reducing grievances from 5–10 per month to only
one in last 10 months.

PLANT MANAGER, Cincinnati Can Manufacturing   1988–1991
Responsible for overall operation of a $60M profit-and-loss can
manufacturing plant, including manufacturing, distribution, human
resource development, financial control. Reported to the Vice-
President/Director of Operations. Plant employment ranged from 200–245
operations employees with a staff of 22 managers and professionals. Products
produced included three-piece cans and ends for four processing plants.
Promoted to return plant to profitability, and develop and implement
management practices consistent with Standard's philosophy.

Major Accomplishments: Attained plant profitability turnaround in first year
of over $2.1M. Achieved productivity improvements exceeding 50% in first
20 months. Virtually eliminated quality complaints from customer plants.

PLANT SUPERINTENDENT/OPERATIONS MANAGER
Tanker-Collins Division   1985–1988
Responsible for production, warehouse/shipping, maintenance and product
control in an 85-machine nonunion plastic processing operation. Plant
employment ranged from 650 to 900 operations employees with a staff of 40
managers and professionals.

M.B.A., University of Pennsylvania, 1974
B.S.M.E., University of Detroit, 1971

EMPLOYMENT SITUATION:

Sandy had earned an accounting degree seven years ago and worked as a controller, bookkeeper, and executive secretary. She had an outgoing personality and felt hampered and lonely doing accounting. She wanted to move into sales and marketing, or supervision. She enjoyed her small rural city, and did not wish to relocate.

STRATEGIES FOR SUCCESS:

Sandy revisited her counselor at her former college placement office, and showed him her chronological resume. Typically her potential employers looked at her accounting jobs and couldn't envision her in sales. Her counselor changed her resume to a functional format putting sales/marketing at the top. She was proud of her accounting accomplishments, so they were listed in the center under Record-Keeping. Supervision was listed last.

COVER LETTER STATEMENTS:

I understand you'll soon be opening a large electronics store at the Westfield Mall. I'm enclosing my resume, as I would like to interview as a candidate for sales manager. I have a background in camera and video equipment sales, and have promoted my college through recruiting activities. I also have a degree in Accounting/Finance, and seven years' experience as a bookkeeper/controller that would be an added advantage to your store's management. I'll call you shortly to see if there's a convenient time for us to meet.

CRITICAL VIEWPOINT:

Sandy had lived in the area for four years, and become very involved in volunteer community affairs. As a result, she had a powerful network of friends that helped connect her to possibilities in sales and marketing. Her counselor reported that Sandy landed a dream of a job within ten days of completing her new resume.

SANDRA McLAUGHLIN
Rt 2, Box 673
Princeton, WV 24740
304/555-9029

SALES AND MARKETING:

- Assisted in the planning and implementation of several Open House Weekends for 150–250 prospective college students.
- Conducted campus tours and interviews with prospective students and their families.
- Planned and implemented a dealership service clinic for 45 current and prospective customers.
- Prepared a marketing cost-effectiveness study for a college Admissions Office.
- Sold cameras and video equipment on a retail level and averaged in the top third among the sales staff.

RECORD-KEEPING:

- Maintained the accounting records and prepared monthly financial statements for a company with five separate profit centers and average annual gross sales of $19,000,000.
- Prepared payroll and maintained records for 75 employees.
- Prepared monthly and quarterly financial statements for five different companies.
- Reconciled daily cash reports for a hotel and restaurant with average daily sales of $8,000.

SUPERVISION:

- Supervised a staff of 38 waiters and waitresses for large banquets.
- Trained, scheduled and supervised a staff of up to 30 campus tour guides.
- Managed a business office staff of four bookkeepers and computer operators.

WORK HISTORY:

1984–Present
BOOKKEEPER/CONTROLLER :

R.K. Denver & Co.	Princeton, WV
Reddy's Oil Change	Princeton, WV
Wappinger Chev/Buick	Staunton, VA
Prestige Toyota	Boca Raton, FL

1981–1984 :
SALES MANAGER :

Cassidy Photo	Tallahassee, FL
Laker Properties	Tallahassee, FL

EDUCATION:

B.A., Accounting/Finance	Davis & Elkins College	Elkins, WV

EMPLOYMENT SITUATION:

Roxanne wanted to make an internal move from account executive to product manager in a company that had carefully structured job descriptions. This company was so large that internal career moves were as competitive as any jobs on the outside. To achieve her goals, Roxanne needed to do good preparation and be willing to call in outside help.

STRATEGIES FOR SUCCESS:

Roxanne's supervisor didn't support her career change, so Roxanne hired an outside counselor. He had her solicit job descriptions from the personnel office for both account executive and product manager. With a full functional description of her desired job, she then needed only to rephrase the description of her past work to fit the requirements of her new target.

She wrote a targeted resume, focusing on her accomplishments in language free of jargon.

COVER LETTER STATEMENTS:

[Internal Memo]

I have studied the Product Manager position, informally interviewing several associates in that function, and I've concluded that my skills are a first-rate match for the position opening soon. I am seeking the opportunity for an interview as soon as possible since the demands of my current position will escalate with the oncoming planning season.

I believe that my outstanding selling skills and my understanding of telecommunications products would add greatly to your department's overall success. I have won awards in college alumni fundraising, and held PTA offices for more than seven years. My off-hours interests are rich and varied, and enhance the skills I can offer you.

CRITICAL VIEWPOINT:

Roxanne's counselor was smart to have her keep her resume simple and highly focused. Her accomplishments translate very well without added detail. Her next step is to keep in touch with the product manager supervisor until she can schedule an interview.

ROXANNE MILLER
428 El Camino Real
Palo Alto, CA 94306
(415) 555-6864 (H)
(415) 555-9375 (W)

JOB TARGET: PRODUCT MANAGER

CAPABILITIES:

- Manage significant amounts of annual revenue.
- Provide telecommunications management, sales, design and implementation functions on the job.
- Effectively communicate and provide interpersonal skills with all levels of business customers and management.
- Manage details under pressure in complex and competitive environments.

ACCOMPLISHMENTS:

- Managed $6.5 million of Pacific Bell revenue.
- Maintained 120% of annual objective in 1989, 1991, 1992 and 1993.
- Managed 110 new business customers to maximize market share.
- Received outstanding sales awards for creating $1.5 million in new revenue.

EXPERIENCE:

1984–Present PACIFIC BELL TELEPHONE COMPANY   Burlingame, CA

1987–Present **Account Executive**
BELL COMMUNICATION SYSTEMS

1984 –1987   **Customer Sales Representative**
Systems Design and Implementation

1982–1984   **Store Manager—THOMPSON'S GIFTS**   Palo Alto, CA

1979–1982   **Department Manager —LIEBERMAN'S**   Menlo Park, CA

EDUCATION :

Over 20 Pacific Bell technical and management training courses

B.S. in Business/Marketing   San Francisco State College

EMPLOYMENT SITUATION:

At his wife's urging, Charles had left a successful career with an insurance company to join her father's business. He learned the business from the bottom up, and his father-in-law planned to turn it over to Charles upon his retirement. Within six years of joining his father-in-law's business, Charles's wife asked him for a divorce and requested that he leave the company as well.

STRATEGIES FOR SUCCESS:

Facing divorce and job-loss at the same time, Charles had emotional issues to work through even before he could start to write a resume. When he finally closed the door on his losses, he discovered that he wanted to return to facilities planning in a large corporate environment. With his career advisor, he assembled a functional resume that could highlight his job of six years ago.

COVER LETTER STATEMENTS:

I believe I can be an asset in addressing your issues around the upcoming plant relocation. Bruce Halverson explained to me that you are facing a critical need, but have no authorization to hire additional permanent employees at this time.

I propose that my services (on a contract basis) during the move would be extremely valuable. My extensive experience in space planning and procurement, along with my managerial background, would enable me to handle a variety of issues for you. My willingness to work on a temporary basis would give you the opportunity to judge the quality of my skills, while meeting the short-term demands of your relocation.

CRITICAL VIEWPOINT:

Charles's marketing strategy worked for him. He is currently working on a six-month contract with a major manufacturer as a facilities planner, and is slotted for an upcoming permanent position. This was an intelligent strategy that allowed him and his targeted company to try each other out.

(Second page covers work history and education. He had no degree, so he listed all his extra course work.)

CHARLES MINNETTO
6321 Pinchot Ave. West
Phoenix, AZ 85033
(602) 555-7470 (h)
(602) 555-8666(w)

MANAGEMENT/ADMINISTRATION

- Interviewed and hired new employees, conducted annual performance evaluations, wrote appraisals and administered salary increases and promotions.
- Forecasted personnel, equipment and space requirements and compiled annual budget.
- Created and implemented problem-solving techniques and procedures and developed efficient record-keeping systems.
- Supervised 20 employees responsible for diverse administrative service functions.
- Organized and conducted sales and safety meetings for subordinates including OSHA compliance, and safety checks of buildings, tools and motor vehicles.
- Designed and developed source materials and reference guides, and instructed safety classes for company of 500 employees.
- Designed and implemented parking program and space allocation for 500 employees.
- Assured project compliance including performance deadlines for state and federal contracts.

SPACE PLANNING/PROCUREMENT

- Assessed equipment and furniture requirements and executed purchase contracts with vendors.
- Bid outside services and contracted for jobs valued in excess of $350,000.
- Maintained optimal warehouse inventory levels on all major industrial, electrical product lines including Toshiba and Texas Instruments.
- Responsible for purchasing all production materials for two full-time shifts of 75 employees.
- Coordinated all arrangements for building moves and 500 employee relocations including a new dimension telephone system without interruption of routines and customer service.
- Planned for efficient and cost-effective use of space, considering user requirements, air conditioning, lighting, furniture and electrical specifications.
- Served as liaison between management, outside vendors and staff on all inter- and intraoffice projects including communications and computer systems.
- Responsible for planning, organizing and executing office relocation of 475 employees into 120,000 s.f. of new office space.
- Scheduled and oversaw construction of 12,000 s.f. computer facility including electrical and climate controls and dedicated lines for two IBM mainframes.

TECHNICAL

- Obtained city and state permits and prepared detailed job prints and contract modifications for completion of construction.
- Investigated equipment failures and recommended cost-effective and expedient repair methods.
- Analyzed equipment orders engineered by consulting firms for compatibility and effectiveness.
- Developed and implemented office supply ordering system and designed maintenance/repair forms.
- Analyzed, purchased and shipped electrical products based on customer requirements.

ELECTRIC ASSOCIATION OF ARIZONA, Phoenix, AZ
  - Electric Motors and Controls

EMPLOYMENT SITUATION:

Dave had been in quality assurance for over twenty years and felt he had reached a dead end. He was halfway through an M.B.A. program and wanted to reassess his interests and accomplishments to see if he could design a new and viable career for himself.

STRATEGIES FOR SUCCESS:

Dave's career counselor had him complete a skill/interest analysis of his full-time work experience and his part-time work in the Navy Reserves. Through this process, Dave soon discovered he wanted to work in industrial training. His counselor had him choose four key words that would appeal to the field and to organize his resume around those four words: research, manage, train, publish. Dave studied the field by reading professional trade magazines and interviewing third-party contacts. Finally, he volunteered to serve on the hospitality committee of the local professional training association.

COVER LETTER STATEMENTS:

I'm considering a change in title, but not necessarily in function. As a training coordinator, I can fully utilize my abilities in teaching, writing, and researching in the development and administration of corporate training programs for your company.

CRITICAL VIEWPOINT:

Dave's strategy worked. Through his many contacts at association meetings, he landed a job in four months. This is another good example of the positive effects of taking action. Volunteer work is a most effective way to network. Through volunteering Dave learned all the "field" jargon and made friends who introduced him to potential employers. Dave edited his resume to include *only* those facts that contributed to the new career, making it short and to the point. A targeted format would have worked equally well.

DAVID JOEL MISASI
4348 West Hacienda Road
Burlingame, CA 94010
(415) 555-7893 (h)
(415) 555-5402 (o)

**DEMONSTRATED
ABILITIES:**

RESEARCHED AND COMPLETED Navy Quality Assurance
Procedures, and translated military jargon into clear expository prose for instruction.

Results: Publication of the first Navy-wide Quality Assurance training
manual.

MANAGED QUALITY CONTROL DEPARTMENT of a major government contractor
including recruiting, training, and evaluating new employees.

Results: A dramatic decrease in quality problems and the lowest employee
turnover in the company.

TRAINED NEW EMPLOYEES in quality control inspection techniques.

Results: Many former employees were promoted to higher-level technical
and management positions.

CONDUCTED TRAINING SESSIONS in Quality Assurance for eight years.

Results: Over 500 reserve and regular Navy personnel attained
professional qualifications resulting in a Navy unit commendation.

PUBLISHED ARTICLES of civic interest for two local newspapers while
publicity chairman of a local jaycee chapter.

Results: Articles instrumental in making projects known to the local
community; participation increased.

EXPERIENCE:	Quality Assurance Specialist **GARDNER ASSOCIATES**, Menlo Park, CA	1982–Present.
	Quality Assurance Supervisor, Instructor, and Admin-Assistant **U.S. NAVY RESERVE**	1979–Present.
	Quality Control Supervisor and Laboratory Research Technician **QUACO INC.**, San Jose, CA	1971–1982.
EDUCATION:	Candidate for M.B.A. —U.C., Berkeley—60% complete Bachelor of Arts degree in Economic Geography—San Jose State University	

EMPLOYMENT SITUATION:

Molly's work history meandered from working as a chef, to teaching, to university research. She had plenty of schooling, including an M.S. in education, and was bored in her university research clerk position. She was unfocused about her next job but knew she wanted a change.

STRATEGIES FOR SUCCESS:

Like many others who come to career counseling, Molly never became totally clear about her job target. She liked planning events, so she and her counselor organized a functional resume that would display the many talents she could employ toward that end. Her research experience helped her follow leads on clients in her various areas of interest.

COVER LETTER STATEMENTS:

[Letter targeted to a wedding planner:]

A client of yours, Sophia Hadley, suggested that I contact you.

I believe my varied experience is perfectly suited to planning large weddings. I have planned and executed numerous large and intimate events. As you can see, I am also familiar with organizing musical entertainment, floral arrangements, and decorations. My background with nonprofit organizations has given me a special appreciation for the need to plan events that are elegant, yet economical.

Sophia explained that your staff is currently complete. I would like to meet with you briefly in the event that you should need support in the future, or on a consulting basis.

CRITICAL VIEWPOINT:

Molly is comfortable with educational and artistic institutions and foundations. She will probably be rewarded with high-visibility consulting jobs. She is so creative that, with a savvy business/financial partner, she could start her own small business. Very creative people frequently job-hop for years in areas completely disconnected from their education.

MOLLY MULLIGAN
155 Autumn Avenue
Brooklyn Heights, NY 11208
(718) 555-8031

CREATIVITY/DESIGN

- Developed special programs in arts of the Middle Ages, history of food and gardening.
- Designed decoration materials for culinary exhibition.
- Developed themes for public festivals.
- Wrote and produced performing arts activities.
- Wrote scripts for special events at historical sites, museums and botanical gardens.
- Developed public information materials.
- Designed decorations, including floral, for special activities.

ORGANIZATION/PLANNING

- Organized art exhibitions.
- Researched and established formal garden tours.
- Planned and coordinated performing arts activities.
- Oversaw preparation of food for daily activities and special events.
- Organized New York University's Annual Alumni Day activities.
- Scheduled and coordinated various aspects involved in successful production of parties, special events, performances and festivals.
- Planned and developed itineraries for visiting scholars.

MANAGEMENT/ADVICE

- Advised employers and clients on protocol and etiquette.
- Provided support and advice on image at national women's convention.
- Assisted with implementation of Image Consultant's training programs.
- Provided special education in history, museums, dance, theater, and botanical gardens.
- Managed popular New York (Brooklyn Heights) restaurant and catering establishment.
- Managed, planned and coordinated special catering events, including the opening of the Mellon Wing at the National Gallery.

WORK HISTORY:

1990–Present **Senior Research Clerk**
New York University, New York, NY

1986–Present **Assistant to Director/Executive Board Member**
Medieval Arts Council, New York, NY

1985–1986 **Teacher**
New York City Board of Education, New York, NY

1977–1983 **Chef—Manager—Caterer**
La Petite Minceur, Brooklyn Heights, NY

EDUCATION:

1993 Columbia University—M.S., Education
1988 Barnard College Graduate Program—Medieval History
1985 Columbia University—B.A., Philosophy
1977 Madeline Senese's Modern Gourmet Cooking School—Chef's Diploma
Images Consulting International—Special training in image and presentation

EMPLOYMENT SITUATION:

From the time she left college, with the exception of a three-year job in financial aid at a university, Jennifer's whole professional career had been in personnel and human relations at the same major corporation. She chose to leave her job and follow her husband to Salt Lake City, Utah, where he had received a faculty appointment. She was looking for any kind of employment that would appropriately use her skills and experience.

STRATEGIES FOR SUCCESS:

Jennifer's career counselor felt a traditional chronological resume would best display her growth in personnel/human resources from specialist to manager. Using italics to emphasize job titles, this format also showed the broad range of her experience that included employee relations, career development, succession planning, training, staffing, recruiting, manpower planning, and other disciplines. This approach provided the widest possible opportunity for potential employers to recognize a fit between Jennifer and any jobs for which they were recruiting. In addition, it allowed the smaller organizations found in Utah to recognize the considerable advantage in hiring an experienced professional with a broad background who was trained in a well-respected company like Jennifer's.

COVER LETTER STATEMENTS:

I am looking for an opportunity to contribute the diverse skills and experience developed during my years at Worldwide Dynamics to an organization that wants its employees to be the very best.

I received excellent training from my company that I would be able to utilize in resolving the critical human resource issues currently facing your organization. My broad background in personnel and human resource disciplines should be useful to you in guiding your work force toward higher satisfaction and performance.

CRITICAL VIEWPOINT:

Although Jennifer's entire strategy was based on promoting the already excellent image associated with her company, for her, it was tantamount to having a great business school degree.

Jennifer B. O'Connell
797 Swanner Place
Salt Lake City, UT 84401
(801) 555-3564

1987–1993	**WORLDWIDE DYNAMICS COMPANY**	
1991–1993	**Corporate Research and Development Center**	Albany, NY

1992–1993   *Manager, Employee Relations Programs*
- Provided comprehensive employee relations support to approximately 1,000 technical and professional employees.
- Introduced and managed new career development training program for employees.
- Administered annual manpower review.
- Supervised eight employees.

1991–1992   *Administrator, Organization and Staffing*
- Administered annual manpower and staffing review.
- Developed management candidates' slates.
- Designed programs with local schools to enhance science and math education.

1987–1991   **Farmington Atomic Power Research Laboratory**   Troy, NY

1990–1991   *Supervisor, Professional Recruiting*
- Hired 160 engineers and scientists.
- Coordinated campus visits for 60 WD recruiters.
- Completed U. S. Government audit of recruiting practices with successful outcome.
- Supervised five employees.

1989–1990   *Specialist, Education and Training*
- Managed $1/2 million budget.
- Administered technical and nontechnical training programs for laboratory personnel.
- Administered tuition refund program.
- Provided career counseling to employees.

1987–1989   *Specialist, Recruitment and Placement*
- Sourced, recruited, hired, and oriented new B.S., M.S., and Ph.D. technical employees to the laboratory.
- Set starting salaries.
- Completed staffing analyses.

1984–1987   **LANGLEY TECHNICAL INSTITUTE**   Schenectady, NY

Assistant Director, Financial Aid
- Completed needs analyses.
- Awarded aid packages.
- Counseled students and parents regarding eligibility.
- Responded to problem correspondence for Director and President.

EDUCATION:

1984	**State University of New York**	New Paltz, NY
	M.S. in Personnel and Counseling	
1982	**State University of New York**	Binghamton, NY
	B.S. in Psychology and Elementary Education	

EMPLOYMENT SITUATION:

Ellen realized she would never achieve partnership in her regional consulting firm. Rather than stay in her current position, she chose to move into private industry, building on her base of very marketable skills. She also wanted to remain in the same geographical area due to family responsibilities.

As a woman in operations improvement consulting, Ellen was a pioneer who enjoyed a solid network in her state of Florida.

STRATEGIES FOR SUCCESS:

Ellen highlighted, in some detail, her impressive accomplishments at a number of companies typical of her market. She had had other kinds of experiences, but her resume was deliberately focused on the needs of manufacturing/distribution companies experiencing healthy growth. Ellen's interview rate was excellent, as CEO's were intrigued at the prospect of picking her brain and/or creating a position for her if they could see a substantial return on their investment.

COVER LETTER STATEMENTS:

My colleague, Frank Everett, has told me about your firm's rapid growth and the complex challenges you face.

As a hands-on operations executive who has resolved similar problems for several Tampa-area manufacturing/distribution companies, I'm seeking to make use of the expertise I've gained in the past fifteen years. My resume details some of the results I've obtained for companies facing similar problems. Frank said you're receptive to new ideas and anticipate aggressive growth in this decade. I'd like to be a part of making that happen.

CRITICAL VIEWPOINT:

The above cover letter was typical of those sent to a target list of mid-market manufacturing/distribution companies in the Tampa/Orlando area. She was very well received.

(Second page covers previous eight years with two companies, her education/accreditation, and her professional and community activities.)

ELLEN K. PETERSON
619 Canal Point Way
Tampa, FL 33606
(813) 555-1432 (Office)
(813) 555-0950 (Home)

OBJECTIVE:

Senior Manager in a high-growth, quality manufacturing/distribution company.

SUMMARY:

Entrepreneurial senior operations executive, with 15 years managing and executing strategic marketing and financial planning, information technology, operations and productivity improvement, and management reporting systems.

PROFESSIONAL EXPERIENCE:

1986–Present   **STONE & RIVERA, INC.**   Tampa, FL

Director - Management Consulting Services

Managed and built a start-up $3 million management consulting business. Expertise includes information technology systems, resource productivity, profit improvement and corporate planning. Served the manufacturing/distribution, telecommunications and health-care industries. Developed business/marketing plans, designed human resource systems, managed a staff of 24 professionals.

- Conceived sales and distribution plans, compensation incentives and expansion strategy for a $500 million Swiss-owned health-care products distributor. Managed the development team and performed the quality assurance for a one million dollar systems-integration project, resulting in over $425,000 annual savings.

- Directed the design and implementation of information technology systems in major telecommunications companies with applications in operations, sales call reporting, product costing, expert systems, and electronic data interchange.

- Developed Just-In-Time manufacturing practices for a nationwide consumer products manufacturer as part of a business turnaround, resulting in reduced cycle time from ten to three days.

- Identified operations improvements in all functional areas of a medical products manufacturer, including total quality management, customer service, and product costing. Developed financial accounting and reporting systems, saving $250,000.

- Served on Governor's Blue Ribbon Panel to improve operations of a statewide health-care system. Recommended financial reporting and information systems changes to improve patient care.

Tampa Chamber of Commerce—Finance Committee

EMPLOYMENT SITUATION:

Ronald was looking for a detective supervisor's position in a small town. He had never used a resume and was completely unfamiliar with job-search techniques. Every job he had held previously was found by chance—he was just in the right place at the right time.

STRATEGIES FOR SUCCESS:

Ronald's counselor decided that Ronald's profession required a chronological resume. It took a long time, however, for Ronald to detail both his duties and his accomplishments. His counselor quizzed him on a typical day, week, month, and year in the life of a police officer. Ronald felt he simply did what a cop is supposed to do, and everybody knows what that is!

COVER LETTER STATEMENTS:

I would like to meet with you to discuss my qualifications and the value that I would be able to provide as your new detective supervisor.

I have carried a good deal of responsibility with the San Francisco Police Department, much of which was drug-related. I understand that drugs have recently become a threat to the well-being of your community. I have some thoughts on ways that you might put a stop to this problem before it grows out of control. I would appreciate some time with you to discuss a few innovative solutions.

CRITICAL VIEWPOINT:

Ronald's resume is clear and simple and gives him the class he needs to move into supervisory work. Supervisory police work is a competitive field and certainly demands good job-finding techniques, including excellent resumes and cover letters.

Ronald Petruzzo
4252 Fulton Street
San Francisco, CA 94101
(415) 555-7998

EXPERIENCE:

1986-Present Office of the District Attorney   San Francisco, CA
DETECTIVE INVESTIGATOR
Conducted more than 200 field investigations, making 78 arrests. Execute orders of the Supreme Court. Execute search warrants. Interview complainants, witnesses, defendants and possible defendants. Prepare initial follow-up and final reports. Participate in surveillance. Testify before grand juries, courts and legislative bodies. Provide protective custody of witnesses. Conduct crime scene searches. Seek, obtain and verify written instruments. Maintain liaison with other governmental and private agencies. Travel out of state and country to locate and secure witnesses and to transport prisoners to local jurisdictions.

1988-Present Office of the District Attorney   San Francisco, CA
FIREARMS INSTRUCTOR
Train and qualify all newly hired Detective Investigators. Upgrade skills and qualify currently employed Detective Investigators three times a year.

1985-1986 Sanders Pontiac, Inc.   Burlingame, CA
SALES REPRESENTATIVE
Sold new and used automobiles. Assured proper expedition of merchandise order from sale to customer delivery. Worked with factory personnel to resolve delays.

1982-1985 Security Police   San Francisco, CA
INVESTIGATOR
Worked as supervisor of investigations directly under the company president. Managed all field operations for over 200 security officers. Screened and hired all employees. Trained all security staff. Issued and monitored equipment. Assigned posts and coordinated scheduling. Monitored activities of all security staff. Investigated internal pilferage cases. Directed activities and performance ratings of all plainclothes officers. Conducted surveillance of assignments and worked as overall troubleshooter.

1977-1982 Various Law Enforcement Positions

EDUCATION:

San Jose State College   B.S.—Criminal Justice

Smith & Wesson Academy—1988   Firearms Instructor's Certification

San Francisco Police Academy—1982

Special training in: Investigative Techniques
                      Criminal Procedure Law
                      Penal Law

EMPLOYMENT SITUATION:

Jessica wanted to continue teaching, but switch to a different environment. She wrote up a laundry-list resume. It was arranged by chronology—dates, schools attended, positions and names of schools at which she had worked, their addresses and phone numbers. This resume was a perfect example of no real facts about duties, much less skills or accomplishments.

Jessica was changing from a parochial to a secular school system, where dates for interviews are posted publicly and candidates arrange for an appointment time by phone. Resumes are sent ahead of the interview.

STRATEGIES FOR SUCCESS:

Jessica's counselor helped her to emphasize the actions and solutions of her work activity. Jessica needed to highlight her achievements—not just her duties—in her resume. She also needed to eliminate religious references.

COVER LETTER STATEMENTS:

I have specialized in teaching reading in the primary grades, and I have experience in teaching elementary mathematics at all levels. I know that your school is particularly interested in providing your students with solid basic skills. I have time at the end of the school day to devote to private tutoring at a very nominal cost. The advantage of my tutoring is that I can communicate directly from within the school with any teacher and/or parent seeking this extra help for their children.

CRITICAL VIEWPOINT:

Although Jessica didn't need the resume to get the interview, by engaging a counselor and working to detail a full, rich picture of herself, she automatically set herself up for a better interview. She walked in having already presented herself in an effective and powerful way. Also, the process of preparing her resume helped her to express herself clearly during the interview.

JESSICA POTTER
1438 Linden Place North
Chicago, IL 60647
(312) 555-3499

TEACHING EXPERIENCE:

ST. SEBASTIAN SCHOOL, Chicago, IL   1988–present

Design lessons and instruct in all subjects appropriate for grade level. Adapt and create learning materials to meet the needs of diverse student competencies. Organize career week for fifth grade class, recruiting community workers as speakers. Plan and accompany students on field trips. Provide interesting activities for special holidays and ethnic celebrations as approved by the board curriculum. Science includes timely information, such as communicable disease awareness and prevention.

Write illustrated class newsletter for open and frequent communication with parents. Maintain attractive classroom, meaningful bulletin boards, and special learning areas.

Received "superior" rating in management, leadership and creativity from school principal.

CHICAGO BOARD OF EDUCATION   1987–1988

Substitute Teacher. Implemented lesson plans as provided by permanent teacher to promote continuity.

CHICAGOLAND MARITIME MUSEUM   1987–1988

Instructor and Tour Guide, Historical and Scientific presentations to all age groups. Trained Instructors in content and procedure.

PROFESSIONAL GROWTH:

Participated in Workshops in Language Arts Methods, Creative Writing, Ethics, Learning Disabilities, Promotion of Appropriate Behavior and Courtesy, Classroom Management, and Arithmetic Methods.   Archdiocesan Schools of Chicago,   1988-1993

VOLUNTEER ACTIVITIES:

Sunday School Teacher, St. Timothy's (1 year)
Bible School Teacher, Bethesda Lutheran Church (2 summers)

CERTIFICATION:

Chicago Board of Education, Elementary
Illinois State Board, K-9, Type 3
Archdiocese of Chicago, Elementary

EDUCATION:

UNIVERSITY OF ILLINOIS, Urbana—B.S.
Elementary Education, Early Childhood Major

EMPLOYMENT SITUATION:

Sarah had a very diverse background that began with teaching and had recently expanded into career and psychological counseling. Her skill in group leadership encouraged her to expand into community relations work. Her long-range goal was to run for political office in her local district. She needed to pull together all the threads of her work experience into a cohesive whole that established her solidly in community relations.

STRATEGIES FOR SUCCESS:

Sarah wrote a combination functional/chronological resume and a powerful cover letter. Her target employer was the Milwaukee Police Department, which was suffering from a severe trauma to its public image.

COVER LETTER STATEMENTS:

I see your recent setbacks as great opportunities for intelligent public–community relations. Part of the problem seems to be that the police don't yet know how to be interviewed by the media. With careful training they could come to understand the need to either choose their words carefully or to avoid interviews altogether.

I perceive the need for ongoing stress-reduction/communications training. I am a trained teacher (Milwaukee Schools), a psychological and career counselor (private practice), and an experienced and popular public speaker. I know that I could design a multifaceted counseling/training program to suit your needs, and could also organize your staff to run it for you.

CRITICAL VIEWPOINT:

Sarah found her target market and tied all the loose ends of her background together, so that her resume would thoroughly support the boldness of her cover letter. In most resumes, such a long list of diverse jobs would be consolidated to avoid confusion, but in Sarah's case the display of diversity worked to her advantage.

SARAH RANDALL
1438 Linden Street PH-B
Milwaukee, WI 53209
(414) 555-7998

CAREER OBJECTIVE: COMMUNITY RELATIONS/PROGRAM DEVELOPMENT

PROVEN SKILLS AND SPECIAL KNOWLEDGE:

• Developed innovative program planning and community contact including: setting objectives, scope and sequence, designing resource retrieval systems, promotional slides, brochures; enlisting community advisory council, project consultant and on-site mentors.

• Maintained and updated records, wrote staff reports, and news press releases, enlisting and using feedback. Determined timeline and budgets. Selected materials and equipment, orienting visitors and convention delegates in program designs; handled in-house staff training stimulating performance and involvement.

• Respond sensitively to clients' needs, acting decisively, delegating as needed and performing with high energy; work in self-directive fashion with diverse groups and as a team member; oriented to problem-solving adaptable to changing circumstances; empathetic, caring, tactful, warm, ethical; inspiring public speaker, instilling enthusiasm and interest; strong abilities in business marketing and negotiating; adept writer; sensitive to the arts.

EXPERIENCE:

1991–present	**Counselor/Consultant** in private practice: personal counseling and consulting
1991–present	**Instructor**, St. Stephen's College, Milwaukee
1986–present	**Vice President** – Board of Directors, Karen Horney Center, Milwaukee
1989–present	**Published Author** in field of psychology; public speaker to various business groups
1991–1986	**Career Development Coordinator and Counselor**, also Business Specialist Instructor, Milwaukee Public Schools
1981–1986	**Board Member**, Milwaukee Board of Realtors
1981–1986	**Adult Education Instructor**, Allied Realtors
1971–1981	**Social Studies Instructor** and **Guidance Counselor**, Milwaukee Public Schools

EDUCATION/CREDENTIALS:

• M.S. Educational Psychology, Guidance and Counseling, from University of Wisconsin, 1975
• B.A. Social Studies, Regis College, Kansas City, MO, 1971
• Wisconsin Professional Counselor License
• Wisconsin Lifetime Teacher's License, Social Sciences

EMPLOYMENT SITUATION:

Pamela was a college graduate with nine years' work experience. She was currently facing multiple problems all at once. After seven years in management at a retail clothing store, she still was making low wages. Her new boss was difficult, and giving Pam a particularly hard time. Pam was also going through a divorce. She wanted to leave her company and to change her industry and her occupation.

STRATEGIES FOR SUCCESS:

When Pamela came to her career counselor, her energy had been depleted. They analyzed her skills and interests in terms of the growing fields in her geographic area. Pamela finally determined that a claims position in insurance would match her preferences and transferable skills. She wrote a functional resume in language that emphasized her past experience in administration, while minimizing retail management.

Pamela's counselor set her up with personal contacts in the insurance industry who interviewed Pamela informally, validating her viability as a candidate. Her confidence and energy grew.

COVER LETTER STATEMENTS:

Hal Goodman suggested I contact you regarding your claims department which has been expanding since your recent merger with Whitman Brothers.

I have excellent skills in customer service, and a good way of absorbing and organizing details. I also have first-hand experience with medical insurance claims, having worked in a busy clinic with over 800 patient visits per month.

CRITICAL VIEWPOINT:

Pamela persevered in her campaign, landing a claims trainee position with a major insurance company. She accomplished her career objectives and opened up a new feeling of accomplishment that helped her face her "life issues" with more strength.

PAMELA J. SMITHERS
17 Oxford Place South
Tulsa, OK 74137
(918) 555-4998

OBJECTIVE: INSURANCE CLAIMS EXAMINER/PROCESSOR

RELATED EXPERIENCE:

CUSTOMER SERVICE

- Audit and examine customer orders for pricing and design accuracy. Follow through on orders to insure completeness and on-time delivery.
- Investigate customer inquiries regarding orders and billing; trace orders/merchandise from vendors. Consistently resolve problems to customer satisfaction.
- Make settlements to resolve customer complaints. Use independent judgment to solve problems and maintain customer relations.
- Assist customers, analyze their needs and inform them of available services.

MANAGEMENT

- Supervise up to seven consultants in department. Screen applicants, schedule and assign work, oversee accuracy and follow-through. Conduct annual review.
- Process sales up to $750,000 annually.
- Consistently meet deadlines for numerous sales and billing reports. Utilize CRT for sale and payroll reports.
- Conduct on-the job training, ensuring applications of classroom training in sales techniques, procedures, measurements and product knowledge.
- Coordinate operations with store manager; serve as liaison between departments.

INSURANCE

- Handled all insurance forms processing for clinic patients. Computerized processing for health and automobile medical benefits.
- Maintained contact with insurance companies regarding treatment coverage; submitted insurance claims.
- Attended insurance claims seminars.

EMPLOYMENT HISTORY:

Studio Coordinator, Norwood Department Stores	Tulsa, OK	1986–present
Sales Associate, Fairview Department Store	Tulsa, OK	1985–1986
Office Assistant, Medical Groups Clinic	Tulsa, OK	1984–1985

EDUCATION:

Bachelor of Science in Consumer Sciences, University of Oklahoma, 1984

EMPLOYMENT SITUATION:

Maria wanted an acting career that would make use of her musicianship and dancing. She had only two years of college with a dual major and no professional credits, but plenty of nonprofessional experience.

STRATEGIES FOR SUCCESS:

Maria's counselor used many facets of Maria's performing arts experience to demonstrate a wide range of skills. Her formal education was placed at the bottom of the page to minimize attention to it. The names of plays and numerous lead roles in which she had performed were listed before theater names, again to minimize attention to them. A glossy 8 X 10 photo is attached to the flip side of theatrical resumes. This is the only resume that requires vital statistics as a prominent feature. Cover letters are rarely used in theater, as resumes are dropped off before or after an open-call or agent-placed audition. This sample is an exception.

COVER LETTER STATEMENTS:

[The following was part of a letter sent to a regional professional theater director.]

I am seeking a year-long apprenticeship with your company starting with the new fall season. I am willing to do all assigned backstage tasks, as well as stand in for any ingenue parts for which I might be suited.

I can play guitar, synthesizer, piano, saxophone, and clarinet, and so could provide live music for plays or individual scenes. This can save you the cost of hiring an additional employee.

CRITICAL VIEWPOINT:

Just starting out in show business, Maria was most in need of either an apprenticeship or a "big break" in New York or Los Angeles. She chose to pursue an apprenticeship, and therefore needed to market herself as willing to do any task, from the aesthetic to the ridiculous, to support the good of the production company. Apprentices usually do an endless number of production tasks while working on their technique and learning the ropes of their profession.

Maria's cover letter makes clear her willingness to do the necessary backstage work and to save the theater company added cost.

MARIA TAYLOR
269 Fairmont Place
Burlington, VT 05401
(802) 555-6063 (Home)
(802) 555-2000 (Service)

STATISTICS:
Height: 5" 6"   Weight : 115   Eyes: Green   Hair: Auburn   D.O.B. 4/4/72

SELECTED PREFORMING ARTS ACCOMPLISHMENTS:
- "Miss Firecracker Contest" (Stage Play/Comedy)—Lead Role, Jarnelle, Burlington Group Theater, Ford Fine Arts Center, 1993
- "The Diary of Anne Frank" (Stage Play/ Drama)— Mrs. Van Daan, St. Matthew's Academy Theater, Burlington, VT, 1990
- "The Ugly Duckling" (Stage Play/Fantasy)—Lead Role, Princess Camilla, St. Matthew's Academy Theater, Burlington, VT, 1989
- "Showdown at the Rainbow Ranch" (Stage Play/Melodrama)—Lead Role, Rainbow, New England Regional Theater, Manchester, NH, 1988
- "Teen" (Pop Rock Musical)—Lead Role, Mary, Marshall High School, Burlington, VT, 1988
- "Adventures of Flimsy Kid" (Stage Play/Comedy)—Lead Role, Lois Brain, Marshall High School, Burlington , VT, 1985

SPECIAL TALENTS AND ACHIEVEMENTS:
Local/Regional/State Superior Awards—Duet Memorized Acting (Without Props)
Eight Years Experience: Talents Shows (Musician/Singer/Actress)
Musician: Guitar, Synthesizer, Piano, Saxophone, Clarinet
Guitar/Vocal Training from Recording Artist/Professional Music Teachers
Sang with band—"High Country" (a Professional Group)
Indian/Tap/Jazz Dancing; Horseback Riding (Both Saddle and Bareback)
Write/Speak French and Hindi Languages
Dialects Include: Southern/Eastern/Western; British/French Accents

MODELING/BEAUTY PAGEANTS:
Coordinator and Model for Several Fashion Shows in Local Area
Junior Miss Pageant Overall 1st Runner-Up Award Winner
Junior Miss Pageant: Talent, Physical Fitness, and Modeling Awards
Miss Vermont Lovely Lady Pageant, Overall 1st Runner-Up Award Winner, 1987
Miss Vermont Lovely Lady Pageant: Formal Gown and Talent Awards

SCHOOL PERFORMING ARTS EXPERIENCE:
Vermont Representative—Celebration Choir, Philadelphia, PA
All-State/Tri-States Choir Member (Soprano); President, H.S. Choir
Captain, Cheerleaders Squad; Drill Team Top Award Winner

EDUCATION:
Attended University of Vermont, Burlington, VT 1990–92
Dual Major: Performing Arts/Broadcast Journalism
(Courses: Acting, Music Appreciation, History of Rock and Roll)
Editor, Newsletter for Campus Organization
Graduate, St. Matthew's Academy for Girls; V.P., Student Council

EMPLOYMENT SITUATION:

Tony was an international sales/marketing manager ready to move on to a new industry. He had attained twenty-three years of professional growth in one company, but had no college education. As his industry was declining, he considered all his professional credits untransferable and out of date.

STRATEGIES FOR SUCCESS:

Tony sought a career counselor who could help him present himself proudly on his resume and overcome his overall sense of defeat in preparing to face the competition. His counselor helped him organize a chronological format emphasizing his career growth. They decided to eliminate Education as a heading altogether. The language was kept generic to sales and marketing management to make the industry shift less obvious.

COVER LETTER STATEMENTS:

As an international marketing manager I bring over twenty years of marketing and sales experience to your company. My solid performance and rapid advancement demonstrate that I am able to interact with a variety of clients, both domestic and international.

I am currently seeking a position in an expanding industry, such as the electrical components business, in which my previous experience in electronics can be utilized. I understand that you are currently exploring markets in Africa, where I have many years of sales experience. I would appreciate an opportunity to discuss your current initiatives and how my extensive marketing background could be useful to you.

CRITICAL VIEWPOINT:

Tony studied his target companies, focusing especially on those with international locations or subsidiaries. Each cover letter was individualized to communicate directly to each potential employer. During interviews he stated that his lack of a college degree was irrelevant given his excellent employment record and steady growth of twenty-three years.

ANTHONY TULLEY
499 Binghamton Road
Bridgeport, CT 06612
(203) 555-6643

WORK EXPERIENCE :

1971 to Present : **U.S. ELECTRICALS, Division of Hammond Electric**
Bridgeport, CT

1988 to Present : **AREA SALES MANAGER / ADMINISTRATION MANAGER**

Direct sales and marketing responsibility for the Middle East and Africa. Make four to six sales trips per year ranging from two to three weeks per trip. Assisted in setting forecasts, administering salary planning, and implementing budgets of $2,000,000. Handle direct negotiation of contracts and projects with foreign government municipalities.

1980 to 1988 : **INTERNATIONAL MARKETING SERVICES MANAGER**

Reported directly to Vice-President of International Sales. Managed 16 regional marketing representatives and customer service personnel. Directed and coordinated all administrative functions performed by foreign subsidiaries and offshore sales offices. Responsible for the training, performance evaluations and work load measurements of direct personnel. Established procedures and practices, and administered pricing, credit, financing, and distribution policies. Assisted Vice-President in expense control and budget development. Controlled and maintained incentive and commission policies.

1978 to 1980 : **PRICE ADMINISTRATOR—INTERNATIONAL**

Administered pricing policies on orders, contracts and project bids to meet annual gross profit targets. Analyzed sub-product mix relative to product objectives and the effect on profit and loss. Conducted pricing studies on competitor's product, resulting in price publication changes.

1975 to 1978 : **SUPERVISOR—INTERNATIONAL**

Supervised order entry, customer service, shipping and documentation and inside sales functions. Responsible for product training and education of all personnel.

1971 to 1975 : **CUSTOMER SERVICE REPRESENTATIVE—INTERNATIONAL**

Performed as an inside sales person responsible for customer quotations and order entry. Administered management's policies on credit, financing, and customer claims.

Military Experience : **CONNECTICUT NATIONAL GUARD** (1968-1974)

EMPLOYMENT SITUATION:

For ten years Andy had worked as a buyer in the electronics industry. In addition, he had a music degree and gave occasional professional performances on the cello. Although he did not wish to work full-time as a cellist, he did want to leave the electronics field to launch a career in community arts programming.

STRATEGIES FOR SUCCESS:

Andy's counselor suggested a targeted resume format to support such a dramatic career change. This career change required research into the newly targeted job so that the potential employer would not have to plow through language difficult to apply to his or her own field. Fortunately, Andy had a varied arts background as well as good business experience, so he felt confident in making this career shift.

COVER LETTER STATEMENTS:

I am submitting the enclosed resume for your consideration for the position of Executive Director of Summer Festivals. Having many years of experience in the business community, I feel that I can provide sound fiscal management and leadership abilities to the Summer Festivals.

My arts background includes hosting a classical radio program, organizing a film series, and writing music reviews. Currently, I am involved in the creation of a folk music museum in Taos. My management skills include extensive work with many people and various business organizations. I certainly feel that my capabilities would be an asset to Summer Festivals.

I look forward to the opportunity to meet with you and discuss the services that I could provide.

CRITICAL VIEWPOINT:

Andy spread his campaign throughout the southwest. The above letter was in response to an ad for a job in San Antonio. He found in his interviews that his competitors were often recent graduates with arts management degrees. However, his ten years of business credits helped him compete.

ANDREW J. UBELL
14 El Morro Road
Albuquerque, NM 87109
(505) 555-2349

Job Target: EXECUTIVE DIRECTOR OF COMMUNITY ARTS PROGRAM

CAPABILITIES:

Arts Management
- Develop creative ideas and concepts into concrete plans with realistic goals.
- Organize and present a variety of programs tailored to specific audiences. Ability to perform initial research and analysis; event planning and contracting for talent, facilities, and labor; advertising, program presentation, and program review.
- Select and appraise performance groups based upon critical evaluation.
- Write copy and review layout for advertising pamphlets, posters and press releases.

Business Management
- Act as liaison, presenting goals and objectives to business groups, chambers of commerce, community groups, and schools.
- Develop public relations and advertising in order to successfully manage development campaigns.
- Responsibly execute and balance budget.
- Recruit and direct staff to accomplish specified goals of an organization.
- Negotiate contracts to obtain cost effectiveness.
- Perform market research to identify organizational needs.

ACCOMPLISHMENTS:

Artistic
- Organized film series for community of 10,000 people.
- Wrote cooking column and music reviews for college magazine.
- Hosted classical music program on KLGL, Taos, NM.
- Performed with the Jimmy Kapps Orchestra at Carnegie Hall, 1986.

Business
- Responsible for procurement of more than $8,000,000 of electronic components annually.
- Exceeded established cost standards resulting in savings of $750,000 annually.
- Present monthly operations review to management in tracking business performance.
- Recruited and trained college students to expedite vendor payments.
- Financial Committee Chairman of New Mexico Old Tyme Fiddlers Association.

WORK HISTORY:

1978–Present:	Professional Musician	Cellist
1987–Present:	Senior Buyer	General Data, Albuquerque, NM
1983–1987:	Buyer	Candido Oilfield Services, Taos, NM
1981–1983:	Salesman	Meridian Electronics, Taos, NM

EDUCATION:

1981 B.A. Communications, Central New Mexico State College

INTERESTS:

Music, Skiing, Art, Cooking, and Tennis

EMPLOYMENT SITUATION:

Stephen lost his job when his company restructured, consolidated staff, and relocated from Denver to Los Angeles. For personal and family reasons he wanted to return to the East Coast.

STRATEGIES FOR SUCCESS:

Stephen's overall plan was to target chief financial officers of Fortune 1000 multinational corporations in major Atlantic-coast cities. His resume emphasized his broad, sophisticated, international approach to tax planning, which would be especially attractive to corporations seeking to expand overseas.

COVER LETTER STATEMENTS:

With twelve years experience as tax counsel at two major multinational corporations, I've particularly enjoyed generating substantial savings in operations worldwide. Each country has its own unique tangle of regulations and challenges!

At this time my family and I are seeking to relocate back to our Atlantic-coast roots. I've been impressed with your rapid growth in recent years, and would like to discuss opportunities to contribute my expertise as a member of your team.

CRITICAL VIEWPOINT:

Stephen landed a position in the Research Triangle of North Carolina after having received offers from three companies. He made a list of the pros and cons of each offer, and included his family and a circle of friends in his decision-making process.

(Second page covers additional functional accomplishments under the headings of Domestic Tax Planning and Compliance, Employment History, Education, and Community Activities.

STEPHEN W. WEISS
12268 Mountain Lane
Denver, Colorado 80204
(303) 555-1943

OBJECTIVE:

Tax Counsel with international and domestic tax planning, legal, business and managerial responsibilities.

SUMMARY:

Tax Counsel with twelve years as Tax Planning Director and Counsel for two multinational corporations. Expertise in foreign tax credits, structuring foreign investment in the U.S., tax treaties, offshore holding companies, corporate and consolidated tax returns, IRS audits, acquisitions and divestitures, and development of foreign tax credit software. Managed 18 professionals.

SELECTED ACCOMPLISHMENTS:

INTERNATIONAL TAX PLANNING AND COMPLIANCE

- Advised on tax aspects of operations in Brazil, France and Abu Dhabi, saving $16 million in foreign taxes for U.S. Alliance and $20 million for Interglobal Resources.
- Saved $8 million of U.S. taxes on foreign non-gas income for American Natural Gas.
- Developed programs in Nicaragua and India to save $2.8 million in reimbursement of contractor taxes.
- Consolidated three Mexican Interglobal Resources subsidiaries into one for a tax benefit of $1.7 million.
- Restructured Korean holdings, saving up to $700,000 for a U.S. Alliance subsidiary.
- Saved $550,000 annually by reducing foreign taxes on expatriate compensation.
- Structured overseas manufacturing on trading investments in Italy, Sweden, Hong Kong and elsewhere to substantially reduce U.S. taxes.

DOMESTIC TAX PLANNING AND COMPLIANCE

- Structured plan to utilize $825 million tax loss carry-forward before anticipated ownership change.
- Developed structure to increase Interglobal's cash flow by $95 million and improve U.S. Alliance's after-tax earnings by $125 million.
- Generated plan for creating $140 million of tax loss carry-forward annually through separation of domestic operations.

Tax Committee Chair, Denver Board of Development
Invited speaker at conferences, seminars and professional meetings.

EMPLOYMENT SITUATION:

Harville was an attorney dissatisfied with what he felt was a mundane work load: divorces, personal bankruptcies, real estate, estate planning, and wills. With growing concern about the level and stability of his income, he decided to switch to corporate law but felt blocked by his age and lack of corporate experience. His business background was limited to banking and accounting.

STRATEGIES FOR SUCCESS:

In creating his resume and identifying career strategies, Harville's career advisor concentrated on the corporate work Harville had done in private practice, identifying several cases that could be used. Although these represented only a small percentage of his actual work, they were made the focus of his resume in a functional format. He targeted companies that could benefit from having a full-time attorney.

COVER LETTER STATEMENTS:

You will find that my background in private practice has made me an excellent self-manager. I can take a project or case from beginning to end—identifying goals and guidelines, establishing and meeting deadlines, and handling all aspects of the casework. I can evaluate situations and make independent decisions. I am particularly skilled at comprehending basic legal issues and constructing arguments or strategies to deal with them.

Additional skills include my ability to prepare well-organized and articulate briefs, memoranda, and written opinions that precisely address the application of the law to the facts.

CRITICAL VIEWPOINT:

Harville's strategy led him to create a niche for himself in one company with which he had previously done a fair amount of work.

(Second page covers his experience in individual and estate tax planning, his certifications and affiliations, specific career history, education, and training.)

HARVILLE WESTERMAN
591 Cumberland Place
Jackson, MS 39204
(601) 555-7074

OBJECTIVE: STAFF ATTORNEY—Corporate Setting

HIGHLIGHTS OF QUALIFICATIONS:

- Superior legal knowledge and skills combined with a special talent for identifying and constructing arguments on the key issues.
- Experienced in Taxation and Estate Planning.
- Two years experience in tax work in a Big 8 accounting firm.
- Six years experience in trust work in a bank setting.

REPRESENTATIVE LEGAL ACCOMPLISHMENTS AND EXPERIENCE:

Litigation and Management of Civil Litigation

- Obtained jury verdict of no liability in $170,000 damages case for my client—a plumbing contractor.
- Won appellate court decision reversing $30,000 punitive damages award against my client–a farm corporation.
- Granted summary motion from trial court on behalf of my client—a bank and its president. Damages claimed were in excess of $100,000.

Business and Corporate Legal Counsel and Advice

- Worked as attorney with total responsibility in general matters and in a broad range of specific legal areas, including:

  - collection of over 500 accounts
  - employment contracts
  - environmental concerns
  - foreclosure proceedings
  - unemployment compensation
  - intrastate commerce

- Handled contract and title work for the purchase of a one million dollar company.

- Negotiated a $350,000 buy-out of major stockholders, and am in final stages of conducting a financial analysis for same company in anticipation of a $750,000 merger.

Bachelor of Arts degree in Political Science, UNIVERSITY OF MISSOURI

EMPLOYMENT SITUATION:

Diana was seeking a promotion to management with her current employer. She came to her counselor with a wordy two-page cover letter and a three-page, triple-spaced resume containing only employer information and lists of duties. Her previous work history had been in an unrelated field, and her current employment had been for only eighteen months.

STRATEGIES FOR SUCCESS:

Ordinarily, Diana's counselor would have developed a functional resume to deemphasize her weighty past history as a hairdresser. However, her employer favored the chronological format, so a long list of value statements was developed for the top half of a one-page resume. In a company facing a possible imminent reorganization, Diana had saved many jobs by helping increase voluntary leaves of absence. This was listed at the very top.

COVER LETTER STATEMENTS:

I am writing to you at the suggestion of my supervisor, Sandy Grennan. Ms. Grennan tells me that a management position is opening in In-Flight Service and that there have been some problems with employee morale.

I feel that I am uniquely qualified for this position. I have been working in in-flight administration since 1990. Last year we were asked to initiate involuntary furloughs. I designed a survey identifying fifty employees desiring voluntary leaves. This project was completed in less than three weeks, and helped to save many jobs.

Before coming to work here, I was the new owner of Great Looks Salon in Fort Lauderdale, taking on a staff that had suffered a year of increased hours and decreased income. Morale was poor and we were losing customers. I developed a motivational program that included incentives and monthly group discussion meetings for employees. Our client base increased by 150% within the first three months of this program.

CRITICAL VIEWPOINT:

Diana is well set to compete for management. She may have to explain her short period as a salon owner and an apparent setback to assistant salon manager. These details would be less obvious in a functional or targeted format.

DIANA WIDMAN
316 East 64th Street
New York, NY 10021
(212) 555-8031

EXPERIENCE :

	WORLD CONTINENTAL AIRWAYS New York, NY
1992-Present	**Supervisor Flight Service**—Administration

- Commended for diligent efforts in increasing voluntary leaves of absence, thus decreasing involuntary furloughs.
- Coordinate medical grounding/ungrounding activity and related payroll activity for 3000 New York–based Flight Attendants.
- Maintain attendance records to assure optimal attendance.
- Organize and administer flight service jet emergency training activities in a timely manner adhering to all deadlines.
- Process and authorize special leave-of-absence requests.
- Arrange and award annual vacations for New York base.
- Provide data and assistance to Personnel Supervisors and Flight Attendants concerning appropriate administrative procedures.
- Monitor Flight Attendant visa requirements.
- Write reimbursements for out-of-pocket expenses.

1992   **Flight Attendant**

- Ensured passenger safety by complying with company and FAA requirements.
- Served as liaison between cabin crew members and cockpit crew.
- Quickly identified and responded to individual passenger needs.
- Directed scheduled food and beverage services in a timely manner.
- Conducted pre-flight briefings for flight service crew.

PALMETTO SALON   Fort Lauderdale, FL

1990-1992   **Assistant Manager/Stylist**

- Maintained loyal following of 150 clients.
- Reconciled daily receipts averaging $5000.
- Organized distribution of commissions to seven stylists.
- Purchased and logged inventory.
- Managed schedule of appointments.

GREAT LOOKS SALON   Fort Lauderdale, FL

1989-1990   **Owner/Stylist**

- Raised initial capital to purchase salon.
- Created and administered employee motivational program.
- Led monthly meetings to ensure quality performance and service.
- Supervised staff.

IMAGESTYLE SALON   Fort Lauderdale, FL

1985-1989   **Manager/Stylist**

- Tripled total customer base in three years.
- Doubled personal clients in one year.
- Developed advertising and promotional campaign that increased salon revenue 400% to $160,000 per year.
- Recruited and interviewed stylists.
- Lectured to junior high school students on cosmetology.

EDUCATION :

1990   **Stephenson College**   Hollywood, FL
        A.S. —Data Entry

EMPLOYMENT SITUATION:

Margaret began in merchandising and marketing, but was overwhelmed by the intensity of the industry; she left the field to accept a job in a more sensitive, organized environment. Although the change was meant to be temporary, it lasted for more than three years. Margaret's true interest was still merchandising and marketing and she wanted to return to it, feeling more confident and prepared after a few years away. Although she was safe and secure as a receptionist, Margaret was underemployed and needed to challenge herself again.

STRATEGIES FOR SUCCESS:

Margaret had strong human relations skills, was a good resource for ideas and information, and was excellent in managing detail. Her special project assignments and activities had been more satisfying for her than the simpler tasks generally assigned a receptionist. Her counselor helped her target a job as an assistant in marketing, as a way to reenter a field that had originally burned her out.

COVER LETTER STATEMENTS:

I attended the National Crystal Convention last week and, while there, collected materials on Wedgewood Crystal. I see that you have a sales force of more than 300 representatives.

I have provided marketing support to large numbers of sales representatives. It has been my experience that these people are able to produce far greater results when they have easy access to materials, contacts, and statistics. This is my area of excellence. In addition, I am a good organizer, having planned many special events and promotional activities.

I would like to meet with you to discuss the possibility of joining your firm as an assistant in the marketing department should an opportunity present itself now or sometime in the future.

CRITICAL VIEWPOINT:

Margaret's resume is appropriately designed to get her back into marketing. She is above entry-level even after six years away from marketing. Her age and her other experience, when separated from the title of receptionist, help to upgrade her image, if she's willing to come on strong in person and on the phone.

MARGARET WILSON
89-21 118th Street
Richmond Hill, NY 11418
(718) 555-2346

MARKETING/MERCHANDISING
- Prepared promotional kits.
- Provided merchandising and marketing support to 400 sales reps.
- Compiled and reviewed sales data.
- Made marketing recommendations to employer.
- Developed new product demonstrations.
- Created merchandising and showroom design.
- Sketched design concepts for upcoming product lines.

ADMINISTRATION
- Manage reception center for major publishing firm.
- Screen publication materials for editorial review.
- Make recommendations for publication from submittals.
- Review and determine legitimacy of contest applications.
- Examined garments for adherence to specification.
- Ensured accuracy of computer system for purchase orders.

ORGANIZATION
- Effectively process and direct telephone communications for staff of 125.
- Coordinate and implement mailings and special projects.
- Prepare for special events; maintain executive itineraries.
- Organized conferences and seminars for national cosmetic firm.

COMMUNICATIONS
- Acted as liaison between design, production and shipping departments.
- Train reception personnel.
- Welcome visitors; respond to and direct public inquiries.
- Perform initial screening of job applicants.
- Administer and grade employee aptitude tests.

EMPLOYMENT HISTORY

1990–Present	CONDE-NAST, INC. **Receptionist**	New York, NY
1988–1990	YOUTHSPRINGS SPORTSWEAR **Production Coordinator**	New York, NY
1987–1988	LINDA LIGHT COSMETICS **Marketing Assistant**	Philadelphia, PA
1984–1987	JOHN CAPROTTI DESIGNS **Manufacturing Assistant**	Philadelphia, PA

EDUCATION

1984	BARD COLLEGE B.A.—Merchandising	Annandale-on-Hudson, NY

EMPLOYMENT SITUATION:

Susan was in her mid-fifties with three grown children out of the house. Although she did occasional substitute teaching, she was also seeking a paid consulting niche in her community. Her specialties were influence management, establishing sound office administration, and handling start-up projects for local community groups. She was having trouble differentiating paid consulting from volunteering when she was writing her resume.

STRATEGIES FOR SUCCESS:

Susan's advisor had her put together a biography summarizing the results of Susan's work without any reference to whether her status had been paid or volunteer. Susan made dozens of personal contacts to get meetings at the "board" level or its equivalent. She set her fee at $150 per day, which was half of her worth had she been working for a private business.

COVER LETTER STATEMENTS:

[She used the interview follow-up letter to market herself after her initial meetings.]

Thank you for telling me about your board of directors' decision to associate your older boys and girls with the town's beautification objectives. As we discussed, my prior experience in organizing innovative projects, dealing with officials in town government, and establishing ongoing coordination capability can be very helpful. Among other things, I have:

- instituted and chaired the UNICEF Halloween program through church Sunday schools.

- established a new auxiliary for the Family Center, to provide a paraprofessional support system to supplement the professionals.

- worked with the business managers of several local organizations to control expenses and evaluate program effectiveness.

CRITICAL VIEWPOINT:

Susan wanted some business, but didn't want to work full-time. She still liked doing per diem teaching when needed. As her price was reasonable she received many offers, but she accepted only those that appealed to her pride and sense of service.

Biography ....

Susan Montrose Winters
61 Mulberry Place
Wichita, KS 67212
(316) 555-8364

Susan Montrose Winters
Consultant to Community Groups

For over thirty years, Susan Winters has been a civic leader for a significant number of community organizations. Her expertise lies in both inspiring and managing innovative projects. Among the many to her credit are the following: establishing the UNICEF program which has become self-sustaining and ongoing; establishing with others a still-going Newcomer's Club; setting up a paraprofessional auxiliary for the Family Center in town; organizing an annual symphony benefit; and, resuscitating a homeless shelter.

Recently she conceived of, conceptualized and developed support for creating a local outdoor performing arts pavilion. She spoke before the responsible town boards and obtained permission for allotment of existing park space. She chaired a successful fundraising campaign and committee, netting $300,000. During the construction phase she worked with designers, builders, and all the support contractors. She brought in the project on time and on budget.

Ms. Winters has had extensive experience with management controls and budgeting for community organizations. In particular, the local library's $4 million annual budget requires sensitive coordination with both town officials and the general public. She is currently successfully managing this.

She obtained an undergraduate degree in liberal arts from Stephens College and later, in 1985, received her Master's in Education from the University of Kansas. She has been involved in teaching in nursery school, and is a teaching aide at the Junior High School.

Ms. Winters and her husband reside in the Old Mission section of town. She is an accomplished singer and choreographer, singing with local town choristers and helping with the dance numbers in the local school plays.

EMPLOYMENT SITUATION:

Peter had a ten-year work history with four layoffs and several company closings. He was working in a geographic area very hard hit by the closing down of heavy manufacturing sites in his industry. He'd always been hired on the spot through the recommendations of friends, but now wanted to consider relocation.

STRATEGIES FOR SUCCESS:

Peter's career counselor had him target three new geographic areas and contact the chamber of commerce in each major target city to determine the long-term viability of his industry in its immediate locale. He also obtained the yellow pages of each city's telephone directory to get names and addresses for sending out his resume.

He used the functional format to highlight his skills and deemphasize his multiple job changes. Under the Work History section, he listed only four of the many jobs he had held over ten years. He grouped the four listed jobs under one date, again to avoid emphasizing the multiple changes. He emphasized titles over company names.

COVER LETTER STATEMENTS:

I have studied your market area and understand that the industry there is healthy and viable. I have strong credits from steady employment over the past ten years. My own hometown has been extremely hard hit economically, and as I'm interested in long-term career growth, your company has the appeal of both challenge and security.

CRITICAL VIEWPOINT:

This is the first time Peter has used a resume and organized a job campaign. He contacted employment agencies in his three target cities. As he was relocating, it didn't matter that he left out some of his employers on his resume. He explained this to the employment agencies, and was never asked about it in his job interviews.

PETER WISNESKI
4752 Stevendale Road
Baton Rouge, LA 70819
(504) 555-0584

EXPERIENCE:

ELECTRONICS, MAINTENANCE MECHANICS, REPAIR

- Provided expert mechanical service for automobiles including accreditation testing, transmissions, brakes, electrical systems, heating and air conditioning, engine performance and emissions tests.
- Installed, maintained and repaired diverse acoustic ceilings.
- Performed electromechanical work with precise timing and precision.
- Repaired sophisticated equipment; replaced and maintained air compressors and pneumatic controls.
- Used skills in electromechanics for troubleshooting and repair of switches, wiring, and phototiming devices.
- Utilized skills in fabrication to create furnaces.
- Provided machine maintenance for grinders, rollers; maintained/repaired all levels of used equipment.

SUPERVISION, COMMUNICATION, INTERPERSONAL SKILLS

- Supervised printing and packaging machines as Maintenance Supervisor.
- Fostered cooperation and strong team effort.
- Dealt comfortably with the general public while conducting demonstrations and sales calls.
- Encouraged repeat business through attention to detail and courtesy.

WORK HISTORY:

1983–Present
Silverleaf BMW/Subaru Dealer   Baton Rouge, LA
     PREVENTIVE MAINTENANCE MECHANIC
Goodyear Company   Baton Rouge, LA
     AUTO REPAIRER
Super-Fixt Systems, Inc.   Metairie, LA
     MAINTENANCE MECHANIC
Expocare Corporation   New Orleans, LA
     MECHANIC, MAINTENANCE DEPT.

EDUCATION:

Rockport Engineering Institute   Baton Rouge, LA
In progress : Associate's Degree in Mechanical Engineering

Southeast Motorcycle Institute   Daytona, FL
Graduate, Certified Motorcycle Mechanic—2-year accelerated course

EMPLOYMENT SITUATION:

Murray came to his company twenty years ago as assistant manager. He moved up the ranks to manager only to be let go at the peak of his career when the owner's son was brought in to take over his position. Murray felt personally connected to the store's customers and staff, and wanted to recreate the same position in the same management style with another firm.

STRATEGIES FOR SUCCESS:

As Murray was very comfortable in the automotive field and had a steady work history there, his career advisor suggested the chronological resume. As there were few retail outlets in his geographic area, Murray listed his skills and accomplishments generically so that he could open up general management or administrative opportunities.

COVER LETTER STATEMENTS:

I bring your company twenty-three years' experience in store management, administration, sales of automobile and truck tires (wholesale and retail), sales of brake and front-end repair service, and supervision of service and warehouse departments. My experience includes billing, purchasing, merchandising, light accounting, credit and collection, inventories, and statistical record-keeping. I possess an excellent ability to work with numbers, including computing decimals, fractions, percentages, and sales tax conversion.

CRITICAL VIEWPOINT:

Murray wasn't bitter about his sudden unemployment. He never lapsed into doubt about his own capabilities, so he pulled his resume and job campaign together quickly. He used the three-pronged approach: cold calls, private networking, and ads and employment agencies. He was also able to use a large number of satisfied customers as references.

MURRAY WITIUK
1540 Old Mission Road
Chattanooga, TN 37411
(615) 555-2946

JOB OBJECTIVE:

Managerial or administrative position to include sales, inspection, expediting, purchasing, inventory and quality control.

EMPLOYMENT:

1973–1993   **Halstead Tire Company**   Chattanooga, TN
             MANAGER/ASSISTANT MANAGER

- Directed operation, selling average of $1.5M annually in wholesale/retail automobile and truck tires, and automobile repair service.
- Spearheaded store's growth from $.5M to $1.5M annual sales in two years through conscientious dedication and excellent customer relations.
- Supervised 10 employees in service and warehouse departments.
- Coordinated all phases of operations in sales, service, and warehouse departments.
- Built team spirit and morale with employees through highly visible management and strong rapport with colleagues.
- Interfaced effectively with general public dealing with an average of 50 customers daily.
- Acknowledged by employees for fairness, sense of humor, and conscientious dedication to quality work.
- Achieved outstanding attendance record over 20 years.

1970–1973   **Firestone Tire and Rubber Company**   Knoxville, TN
             ASSISTANT STORE MANAGER

- Gained broad experience in billing, purchasing, merchandising, management, credit and collection, inventory and quality control, statistical record-keeping, and light accounting.

EDUCATION:

UNIVERSITY OF TENNESSEE   Knoxville, TN
Economics, Math concentration; Liberal Arts Program—two years

Company/Military-sponsored training programs in personnel development and office management

EMPLOYMENT SITUATION:

Hal had graduated from college less than four years ago, and held only two short-term positions in newspaper journalism. He had worked regularly all during college, writing articles and publishing a magazine about the music industry. He wanted to continue writing, moving into more serious and meaningful work either in government or an area related to a significant national or international cause. He had developed distaste for newspaper journalism, believing that the news was not being reported fairly and objectively, and that the focus was more on scandal and sensationalism.

STRATEGIES FOR SUCCESS:

The principal strategy was to make a clear presentation of capability, experience, and interest in journalism, and to relate Hal's specific accomplishments in using his writing skills for a bigger purpose.

COVER LETTER STATEMENTS:

My work as an investigative journalist has given me a deep and clear understanding of the issues facing the urban poor today. I would appreciate the opportunity to meet with you to discuss how I can help your agency develop the best possible relations with the organizations that fund you.

As a successful journalist I developed an effective style of writing that might be useful to you in drafting fundraising proposals, public relations briefs, informational articles, and other documents that describe your agency's work.

My research and writing in the pop music industry have given me an insight into the language and culture of young Americans that would be extremely useful in describing your programs for teens to the public as well as to funding agencies.

CRITICAL VIEWPOINT:

Hal had acquired some marketable journalistic credits in college and in his short work history. Notice that the most detailed sentences at the top half of his resume cover his writing about politics, low-income housing, and neighborhood issues. His cover letter focused his purpose even more clearly.

HOWARD ALLEN WOLFSON
454 Harding Place
Chicago, IL 60610
(312) 555-2246

Newspaper Journalism
- Provided regional political reporting for a newspaper with a circulation of 130,000.
- Covered the City of Suffolk, VA including zoning and planning boards, city council meetings, and neighborhood issues.
- Wrote articles on regional issues including transportation, housing, and the economy.
- Reported on court proceedings in five suburban Chicago-area Circuit Court districts.
- Covered U.S. District Court proceedings.
- Reported spot coverage of police, politics, and public relations stories.
- Wrote stories from information supplied by reporters and news releases.
- Served as weekend editor, edited copy, and made daily schedule for wire-service clients.
- Covered Illinois state politics including State Legislature and local political races.
- Developed media strategy and campaigns to attract coverage of housing issues such as the Low-Income Housing Credit and other nonprofit development efforts.

Music Industry Journalism
- Developed in-depth understanding of the pop music industry.
- Wrote feature stories and articles about relationship of pop music industry politics and political culture.
- Wrote live concert and recorded album reviews.
- Reported on record industry news.
- Interviewed musicians.
- Published articles in suburban *Chicago Tribune*, music industry magazines including *Catharsis* and *Jet Lag*, and political magazines.
- Founded, published, and edited a music magazine, *Better Than Anything*, in Urbana, IL.

Work History:
1992–1993	**Suffolk News Daily Press, Suffolk, VA**
	Reporter
1990–1992	**Chicago City News Bureau, Chicago, IL**
1991–1992	*Court Room Reporter*
1990–1991	*General Assignment Reporter*

Education:
1990	**University of Illinois, Champaign-Urbana, IL**
	B.A. Political Science

Part Three

How to Write a Resume: A Mini-Guide

*A simplified step-by-step process
for writing your resume.*

On the following pages you will find an abbreviated course designed to help you put together a great resume. These are resume-writing rules that we have gathered over twenty years of front-line experience with employers, candidates, and consultants. This material is presented in expanded form—with worksheets, examples, and a twenty-six-page job targeting process—in the book *The Perfect Resume* from the same author and publisher (see Resources, p. 202).

The Ten Most Common Resume-Writing Mistakes

Scores of prime employers, career counselors, and employment agencies shared with us what they think are the most commonly made mistakes in the thousands of resumes they see. Here they are:

1. Too long.
2. Disorganized—information is scattered around the page—hard to follow.

3. Poorly typed and printed—hard to read—looks unprofessional.

4. Overwritten—long paragraphs and sentences—takes too long to say too little.

5. Too sparse—gives only bare essentials: dates and job titles.

6. Not oriented for results—doesn't show what the candidate accomplished on the job—frequent platitudes disconnected from specific results.

7. Too many irrelevancies—height, weight, sex, health, marital status are not needed on resumes. Only show business or modeling professionals need this data.

8. Misspellings, typographical errors, poor grammar.

9. Tries too hard—fancy typesetting and binders, photographs and exotic paper stocks that distract from the clarity of the presentation.

10. Misdirected—too many resumes arrive on employers' desks unrequested, and with little or no apparent connections to the organization—really good cover letters will avoid this.

WHAT IS A RESUME?

A resume is an advertisement for yourself designed to communicate your work history in a way that motivates an employer to invite you for an interview.

A great resume is not a biography or memoir. It is not a detailed history of your life and times. Perhaps, surprisingly, it is not even an application for employment. A great resume is a well-structured, easy-to-read presentation of your capabilities and accomplishments.

Is it aggressive, bragging, or immodest? No, not at all. We are continually surprised to run into students, workers, and even career counselors who take the position that job seekers should *underplay* their enthusiasm, avoiding direct statements of personal ability. They suggest substituting the reluctant "I would like to try" for the imperative "I can." Bad advice! If you doubt this, ask how does the organization you are applying to describe *its* services or products? Do they hide their strengths? Play down their capabilities? Obscure their primary accomplishments? If so, we're willing to have you take the soft line. But frankly, we don't know many organizations that do these things. On the contrary, we find that the most productive and exciting organizations have very little hesitancy to let you know who they are and what they do.

We're not talking about *hype* or inflated self-praise or lies. We are talking about a clear, unembarrassed portrayal of yourself, presented in the best possible light. Show the picture of you with all systems Go, and all the stops out. You know what we mean—that side of you that wakes up to the challenge, that impresses your friends and family. That's the person we want you to write about. Leave out the warts and pimples—the times when you turned the wrong corner or forgot to set the alarm.

JOB ATTRACTORS

Here are some of the job attractors, power words, and phrases to favor in this challenging decade:

- your ability to move seamlessly, swiftly, and capably from task to task, one work environment to another, soft product to hard product, and—for high flyers—across national boundaries
- your ability to master new concepts, ideas, and practices
- versatility, flexibility, mobility
- high learning curve
- innovative ways of engaging problems
- organizing and reorganizing new data, work systems, and corporate processes
- working integratively, able to balance divergent functions
- entrepreneurial, and risk-smart
- customer-focused
- cross-cultural
- computer literate
- work on special task forces, project teams
- thinking globally and acting locally
- quality-oriented
- multinational, multicultural
- emphasizing second and third languages—human or data base

Preparing Your Resume

1. TARGET YOUR JOB

A job target is a particular work direction or title in a given field. It is not a specific job opening, but rather a title that could exist with a number of employers. For example: *satellite conferencing rep, cost accountant, travel agent, wellness director.* Your resume will be dramatically more valuable and communicative if it has been fashioned for a job target that you have worked out in advance. Once you are clear about the target, it becomes obvious what to include and what to leave out. *Important:* we are not necessarily recommending that you include your job target on the resume itself, except in the targeted format (see below). But in order to focus and compose the resume you should have a target in mind.

Given the complexity of opportunity in today's work environment, you will probably have two, three, or even four job targets in related or—in some cases—different fields reflecting diverse sets of interests and skills. The basic requirement for a job target is that *it starts with you.* You put it together using your skills and interests. If your job target areas relate only to your skills, your work will miss the essential pleasure bonds that keep the juices of motivation and satisfaction flowing. On the other hand, if you go after areas of interest where you don't have a viable skill base, you won't have much to describe in your resume or interview.

A job target is something at which you aim. It lies along a course line, or lifeline, and can include a short-term job goal as well as long-term career direction. For example, your three-year target could be as an employment manager and your immediate job goal might be as an interviewer or recruiter.

With a clear job target, you are in charge of your work search, and your resume reflects this clarity. The extra work involved in targeting pays dividends in the ease and organization of your job search and resume.

2. CHOOSE A FORMAT

For the best results you should use a form or format that reflects the particular demands or requirements of your own job targets and work history. Although there are many different *layouts*, there are really only four basic resume formats that you need to know. These are the building blocks for all resume styles:

Chronological Format: Work experience and personal history arranged in reverse time sequence. In this resume the job history is shown with the most recent job first and having the most space. Titles and organizations are emphasized and duties and accomplishments within those titles described.

Best used when your career direction is clear and the job target is directly in line with your last employer.

IS advantageous

- when name of last employer is an important consideration.
- when staying in the same field as prior jobs.
- when job history shows real growth and development.
- when prior titles are impressive.
- in highly traditional fields (education, government).

IS NOT advantageous

- when work history is spotty.
- when changing career goals.
- when you have changed employers too frequently.
- when you wish to deemphasize age.
- when you have been doing the same thing too long.
- when you have been absent from the job market for a while.
- when you are looking for your first job.

Functional Format: Work experience and abilities cataloged by major area of involvement—sometimes with dates, sometimes without. This format highlights major areas of accomplishment and strength organized in an order that best supports your work objectives and job targets. Actual titles and work history are in a subordinate position and are occasionally left off entirely.

Best used in cases of career change or redirection, first-job search, or reentry into the job market; effective when you wish to play up a particularly strong area of ability.

IS advantageous

- when you want to emphasize capabilities not used in recent work experience.
- when changing careers.
- when entering the job market for the first time.
- when reentering the job market after an absence.
- if career growth in the past has not been good.
- when you have had a variety of different, relatively unconnected work experiences.
- where much of your work has been free-lance, consulting, or temporary.

IS NOT advantageous

- when you want to emphasize a management growth pattern.
- for highly traditional fields such as teaching, ministerial, or political, where the specific employers are of paramount importance.
- where you have performed a limited number of functions in your work.
- where your most recent employers have been *highly* prestigious.

Targeted Format: A highly future-focused presentation directed to a very specific job target. This format is best for focusing on a clear, specific job target (you would have a different one for each target). It lists future-oriented capabilities and supporting accomplishments that relate to a clear job target. Best used when you are clear about your job targets and what they require.

IS advantageous

- when you are very clear about your job target.
- when you have several directions in which you might go and want a different resume for each.

- when you want to emphasize capabilities you possess, but for which you may not have been *paid*.

IS NOT advantageous

- when you want to use one resume for several applications.
- when you are not clear about your capabilities and accomplishments.
- when you are just starting your career and have little experience.

Creative Combination: A free-form approach that might combine several formats to suit a specific need or personality. Not for everyone, the creative resume abandons customary forms and demonstrates a highly individual approach. Unless extremely well done, this approach can flop miserably. When done with great skill, it works very well.

Best used by people in creative or entrepreneurially open fields.

IS advantageous

- for the fields in which written or visual creativity are prime requisites of the job.
- when the medium of your work is appropriate to a printed form.
- in independent fields.

IS NOT advantageous

- if you are planning to go through personnel.
- if you are not very sure of your creative ability.
- if you are looking for a management position.

Preparing the Chronological Resume

You should choose the chronological resume to highlight a good work history related directly to your next job target, without major gaps or numerous job changes.

Guidelines for the Chronological Resume:

1. Start with present or most recent position, and work backward, with most space devoted to recent employment.

2. Detail only the last four or five positions or employment covering the last ten or so years. Summarize early positions unless exceptionally relevant to the present.

3. Use year designations, not month and day. Greater detail can be given in the interview or application.

4. You don't need to show every major position change with a given employer. List the most recent or present position and two or three others at the most.

5. Do not repeat details that are common to several positions.

6. Within each position stress the *major* accomplishments and responsibilities that demonstrate your full competency on the job. Once the most significant aspects of your work are clear, it is generally not necessary to include lesser ones, as they will be assumed by employers.

7. Keep your next job *target* in mind, and as you describe prior positions and accomplishments emphasize those that are most related to your next move up.

8. Education is not included in chronological order. If it is within the past five years, it should go at the top of the resume. If earlier than that, at the bottom.

9. And, of course, keep the resume clear, crisp, short.

JOHN ANGELO
279 Ralston Road
Richmond, VA 23235
(804) 555-5617

| 1990-1992 | Century Corporate Towers | Richmond, VA |

BUILDING MANAGER

Managed two 12-story twin corporate towers from early construction through completion totalling 700,000 s.f.. Directed activities for all areas:

- Operated heating, ventilation and air conditioning.
- Supervised custodial services including marble restoration.
- Coordinated corporate tenant relocation, completion of tenant suites and additional construction needs.
- Assigned maintenance personnel for building needs.
- Supervised maintenance of two six-level parking garages, corporate park roadways and all entrances.
- Managed all logistics associated with fire detection, emergency generators, security access, elevator systems, inside and outside decorative pools and general ambiance.

| 1960-1990 | Richmond Police Department | Richmond, VA |

1982-1990 **LIEUTENANT**

- Supervised maintenance of Richmond Police Station.
- Prepared budget requests for Support Services Division.
- Directed the installation of traffic signs, signals and road markings.
- Purchased and replaced police cruisers and oversaw the maintenance of entire fleet.
- Managed personnel in Support Services Division.
- Created computer programs for burglar alarms, accident data, and vehicle preventive maintenance systems.

1975-1982 **SERGEANT**

1970-1975 **DETECTIVE**

1960-1970 **PATROL OFFICER**

BOARD MEMBERSHIPS / PROFESSIONAL AFFILIATIONS:

- Richmond Civil Preparedness Advisory Board
- Police Zoning Code Enforcement Board
- Richmond Parking Authority and Community Development Committee
- Accepted as photographer in Chamber of Commerce juried show for past five years
- Building Owners' Management Association (BOMA)

EDUCATION:

| 1978 | University of Richmond | A.S. Criminal Justice |
| | Graduate, FBI Academy | Quantico, VA. |

PREPARING THE FUNCTIONAL RESUME

By selecting the functional resume format, you choose to highlight particular areas of capability in order of highest relevance and potential rather than stay strictly with a chronological work history. By doing this you will be able to point toward selected career directions and play down possible gaps or inconsistencies in past work. If you are changing careers, or entering or reentering the job market, you should choose an approach that will also allow you to easily include nonpaying work experience and school or community activities.

Guidelines for the Functional Resume:

1. Use four or five separate paragraphs or sections, each one headlining a particular area of expertise or involvement (such as Financial Planning, Counseling, Supervision, Research, Sales, and so forth).

2. List the functional paragraphs in order of importance, with the area most related to your present job target at the top and containing slightly more information.

3. Within each functional area stress the most directly related accomplishments or results you have produced, or your most powerful abilities.

4. Know that you can include any relevant accomplishments without necessarily identifying which employment or non-employment situation it was connected to.

5. Include education toward the bottom, unless it was within the past three to five years. If it was in an unrelated field, include it at the end regardless of how recent.

6. List a brief synopsis of your actual work experience toward the bottom of the resume, giving dates, employer, and title. If you have no work experience or a very spotty record, leave out the employment synopsis entirely (but be prepared to talk about the subject at the interview).

7. Keep the length to one or two pages.

JOCELYN CARMICHAEL
8442 Appleton Drive
St. Louis, MO 63132
(314) 555-2100 Messages

OBJECTIVE: CONCIERGE—HOTEL INDUSTRY

COMMUNICATIONS / HOSPITALITY:

- Handled variety of clerical/social functions including reception, entertaining, and making people of diverse interests and economic status feel comfortable.
- Coordinated and oversaw two Ameritech Regional conferences that were highly acclaimed (attended by 2000 and 6000 each).
- Accustomed to accepting responsibility, delegating authority and working with people of all ages.
- Wrote surveys to determine customer ideas; developed correspondence that enhanced customer support and calculated impact of various programs.
- Coordinated many community events including Pace Setter activities.
- Participated in wide variety of diverse activities including United Negro College Scholarship Fund, WBI Person-to-Person Friendly Visit Program, and the Juneau Village Ronald McDonald Charity.

MANAGEMENT:

- Supervised 10 to 15 associates and effectively helped develop careers.
- Assisted in the creation of consumer market education recommendations and new employee orientation programs.
- Initiated and coordinated human resource programs for a broad variety of populations. Acknowledged for outstanding dedication and follow-up.
- Developed projects with attention to detail and timely, cost-effective, high-quality results.

WORK EXPERIENCE:

1962–1992 SOUTHWESTERN BELL TELEPHONE
Various positions, including middle management

1975–Present
Volunteer—Welcome Wagon, March of Dimes, American Cancer Society and others previously listed

EDUCATION:

Successfully completed numerous management and personal development courses.
High School Graduate/Scholarship to Nursing School

PREPARING THE TARGETED RESUME

Unlike the chronological and functional resumes, which describe past work, the targeted resume features statements about what you *can do*—your capabilities—even if you have not actually had any direct relevant experience yet. You are using the targeted resume because you are clear about a particular job target or targets (use a different resume for each) and your willingness to focus on these only. The resume is actually quite simple to prepare, so it would not be difficult on a computer or word processor to put together three or four.

Using this format it is essential to research the fields you have chosen to target. If you are interested in finding out more about your job target areas, a visit to your library is essential. Books, periodicals, reference works, trade publications, and bibliographies will give you insight and direction. Ask the librarian, who can help you find out about what people do in this field, and the jargon they use. You will be able to express truly relevant capabilities that clearly support your targets.

Guidelines for the Targeted Resume:

1. You must be clear about a specific job target (or targets if you plan several versions). A job target is a clear description of a particular title or occupational field that you want to pursue.

2. The statements of capabilities and accomplishments will be short statements of one or two lines, generally written in an active style.

3. Listed capabilities will answer the underlying question, "What *can* you do?" Listed accomplishments will answer the underlying question, "What *have* you done?"

4. List a brief synopsis of your actual work experience toward the bottom of the resume, giving dates, employer, and title.

5. Experience and education are listed but not openly stressed—they support rather than control.

CHRISTOPHER M. KOHL
8562 Lanhart Road
Little Rock, AR 72204
(501) 555-3941

JOB TARGET: MANAGEMENT TRAINEE–MATERIALS MANAGEMENT

CAPABILITIES

- Interview vendors to obtain product information, pricing and delivery date.
- Discuss defects of goods with quality control or inspection personnel to determine source of trouble and take corrective actions.
- Keep computerized records pertaining to inventory, costs, and deliveries.
- Make sound decisions based on personal experience and judgment as well as verifiable facts and data.
- Work long hours without physical stress or annoyance.

ACHIEVEMENTS

- Supervised and coordinated trucking terminal workers' activities and assignments in distribution and loading of goods.
- Inspected shipments for damage, and trained dock workers in correct ways to handle different kinds of material.
- Processed and handled billing documents.
- Handled customer complaints by determining freight location and estimating time of delivery using nationwide IBM communications system.
- Located and expedited rush shipments.

WORK HISTORY

Operations Coordinator
HOLLIS TRUCK LINES, INC.   Little Rock, AR   1992–present

Office Help/Laborer
WOODLEY CONSTRUCTION COMPANY   Little Rock, AR   1988–1992

EDUCATION

Bachelor of Science   Policy and Administration, University of Arkansas   1992

Preparing the Creative Combination Resume

A creative combination resume is an individual stylized message that expresses your skills in an unusual way. The first rule about the creative combination is *not* to take this approach unless you are truly able to put together a level of communication that works well in *the eyes of another*—and that will be so received by the person to whom it is directed. Resume readers are skeptical, and the line between uniqueness and gimmickry can be very obvious to them.

Guidelines for the Creative Combination:

For each creative combination we have seen work, there are five that have fallen flat. Here are some pointers to consider if this approach appeals to you.

1. Consider preparing a more conventional resume as a back-up.
2. Make sure what you do is very professionally produced or reproduced.
3. Make the results look effortless—not a grind.
4. Favor brevity and simplicity.
5. Make sure the point is made: a personal meeting is called for.

We have provided samples of the creative alternative on pp. 33, 51, 61, 75, 85, 151, and 165, since there is no pattern to follow. In this one, *you* are in the writer's seat.

3. DRAFT YOUR RESUME

You will probably want to have a different version of your resume to cover each major direction or job target in your employment search. If you have two or three job targets in the same general field, and you are using the chronological or functional format, then one version will suffice. If your job targets are reasonably diverse, then you will probably want one version for each target. Customized targeted resumes will give you maximum penetration for each target or work title.

Organize the writing of your resume so that the main points you make stand out and direct the reader's attention to the benefits you offer. Keep the writing concise and to the point. Use power words—action verbs—to head off the sentences and paragraphs.

LOUISE FOLEY
17 Dorcas Circle East
Mesa, AZ 85206
(602) 555-2169

JOB TARGET: DEVELOPMENT AND CORPORATE GIVING

FUNDRAISING/DEVELOPMENT/SALES:
- Raised over $170,000 for the ASU School of Music during a ten-year period. Raised $20,000 for a single event this year.
- Increased retail sales for women's boutique by 32% as part-time employee. Was offered own store based on successful retail ability.
- Raised $65,000 in four months for high school band to perform in Fiji.
- Saved organization over $2,500 in insurance premiums through research.

EVENT PLANNING:
- Successfully developed and coordinated six golf tournaments.
- Planned and organized ten "friend-raising" events for ASU School of Music. Other universities used this successful group as a model for their development programs.
- Planned and organized membership and audience development campaigns for nonprofit arts organization.
- Oversaw and promoted various events via print and electronic media, including appearances and interviews.
- Served as President, Board of Directors, ASU Music Circle for two years, supervising 30 active volunteers.

MANAGING/SUPERVISING:
- Served as president of various community organizations, managing groups of volunteers in event and fundraising efforts.
- Served as President of Board of Trustees at church, supervising board of twelve.

SKILLS:
- Speaking Spanish.
- Public speaking.
- Writing and editing.
- Typing, computer literate and learning!

EXPERIENCE:
1988–1993	ARIZONA SCHOLARSHIPS FUND GOLF TOURNAMENT
	Assistant Chair
1983–1993	ASU MUSIC CIRCLE BOARD OF DIRECTORS
	President, 1984-1986
1991–present	FOLEY'S FASHION—Fashion consultant and sales
1989–1991	THE RITZ CLOTHING BAZAAR—Sales
1983–1988	EDITOR—ASU School of Music Newsletter

EDUCATION:
B.S. Cal State University
Workshops in public relations, writing, brochures, development
Spanish Language Certification, U. S./Mexico Institute, Mexico City
Undergraduate and graduate courses in music from Cal State University

Personal Power Word List

Created	Wrote	Referred
Instructed	Analyzed	Served
Reduced (losses)	Produced	Compounded
Negotiated	Conducted	Networked
Planned	Delivered	Observed
Sold	Founded	Studied
Completed	Assisted	Improved
Designed	Leveraged	Consolidated
Consulted	Increased	Ordered
Evaluated	Trained	Invented
Calculated	Supplied	Diagnosed
Identified	Maintained	Examined
Performed	Administered	Lectured
Constructed	Advised	Processed
Controlled	Restored	Reviewed
Dispensed	Critiqued	Translated
Formulated	Realized	Prescribed
Improved	Rewarded	Charted
Tested	Purchased	Represented
Protected	Oversaw	Promoted
Obtained	Installed	Recorded
Programmed	Routed	Operated
Rendered	Corresponded	Supervised
Instructed	Audited	Drew up
Counseled	Coordinated	Organized
Received	Researched	Strategized
Built	Implemented	Expanded
Detected	Presented	Devised
Selected	Instituted	Prepared
Logged	Directed	Interpreted
Recommended	Managed	Interviewed
Distributed	Eliminated	Discovered
Arranged	Provided	Conserved
Disapproved	Solved	Arbitrated
Developed	Determined	Assembled
Edited	Collected	Navigated

4. DESIGN, EXECUTION, AND PRODUCTION

PROCESSING YOUR RESUME

The power of the personal computer, word processor, and now the advent of special software for computer and letter-writing preparation offers you advantages that were rare even a few years ago. Basic word processing alone can cut in half the time for editing, revising, customizing, and updating old or basic resumes. There are many supports you will find right there in your standard word processor.

- Keeping a "stockpile" of powerful resume paragraphs on disk that can be cut and pasted in a variety of combinations to emphasize particular accomplishments or experience.
- Adding new accomplishments or experiences as they happen.
- Trying out your resume in a variety of formats, fonts, bolds, under-lines, left justification, etc., to review—one against the other—in order to contrast, compare, and choose the right one for the job at hand.
- Editing to fit one page or two.
- "Spell-checking" and thesaurus of synonyms.
- Revising in order to expand certain sections over others.
- Using a laser printer for top-quality appearance.
- Keeping a disk-based copy.

Before your resume is seriously read by anyone on the employment cycle, it has to pass what we call the *flash test*—that first three- to four-second look in which the reader decides whether or not it's worth reading any further. This is analogous to the way you decide which articles or advertisements are worth reading.

Unfortunately, in the unfair employment world, our skills just aren't enough—packaging counts. Employers and consultants agree that many able candidates don't make it beyond the initial screening process due to poorly constructed, poorly presented resumes. The underlying assumption is that if you can't communicate about yourself in a way that invites interest and attention, you aren't fully equipped to deal with today's highly communi-cations-oriented work world.

Keep it simple, and clear—not showy or complex. Avoid excessive un-derlinings, bolds, words in all capital letters. If you highlight too much, you have essentially highlighted nothing.

When it comes to printing or duplication, go for the best laser printer, or professional copy shop. Think twice before you use the corner photocopy machine; the stock and the printing they offer are often more convenient than professional. Remember that your resume not only *describes*, it also *demonstrates* your ability to manage good written communication.

5. EDIT AND CRITIQUE

Don't expect to achieve the best layout, styling, and impact on your resume's first draft. Plan to do two or three drafts—either by hand, word processor, or typewriter. Once you have pulled the information together, edit ruthlessly, cutting back sentences that are too long, eliminating redundancies and stylistic confusion.

Get the first or second draft reviewed by someone who is very good at grammar, spelling, and punctuation. Don't plan to do this yourself, as most of us have blind spots about our own errors. Take this critique and editing function very seriously.

When you ask to have your resume reviewed don't present it with a question like "Isn't this a good resume?" or "How do you like this?" Rather say, "Do you have any ideas how to make this stronger?" or "Please look for any errors."

A good critique points out errors and lack of clarity. Avoid discussions of format, content, or emphasis unless the person critiquing is really an expert.

THE STRATEGIC MARKETING (COVER) LETTER

As you have seen in the samples in the previous section, despite the clarity and precision of these resumes and the attention given to the job targets and personal objectives, when all is said and done they remain only printed forms. Even with the highest degree of personalization, the resume is a generalized communication. It remains for the reader to interpret, analyze, and predict how these very real attributes can be put to work for them in the immediate job situation. Sometimes employers make the right interpretations, and sometimes they don't. Once you have produced your perfect resume, a customized cover letter is your best way of multiplying the odds of a direct hit right at the center of the employer's interest.

The purpose of the customized cover letter is to communicate a *specific, personalized* message to a *particular* employer, answering the most fundamental employment question of all: *Why should I hire you?* The cover letter is your way to so distinguish what you have to offer that the likelihood of an interview is at least doubled. Given the complexity and uniqueness of today's job market, the cover letter is an increasingly important tool for the high level of career success you seek. A customized cover letter should go out with each individual resume you send. Given the aptitude of word processors and software, this step is not as difficult as it might once have been. Simply follow these basic rules.

COVER LETTER RULES

1 —Address It to a Particular Person by Name

Send your letter to the person who can make the hiring decision, using his or her name. Personalized letters get read first. Think of your own experience when you open the mail. The letters addressed to you personally get read. The form letter to "sir" or "madam" or "occupant" usually ends up in the trash.

Call the firm at which you want to interview and find out the name (correct spelling, please) and title of the individual in charge of the department in which you would like to work. Don't worry if it takes three or four calls. If you get stuck, call the president's office and find out from someone there who is in charge of your area of interest. Don't say that you are looking for a job. Say you have some information to send and want to make sure it gets into the hands of the right person.

2 —Communicate Something Special

People who get a lot of mail are wary of form letters and have developed personal techniques to skim quickly before reading to see if the letter has a message for them. In your opening lines, write something that is uniquely associated with the person, division, or organization, thus signaling to the reader that you invested the time to communicate personally.

The likelihood of a personal response to your letter is directly related to the degree of personal attention you put into it in the first place. Some typical "personal" openings are:

"I see that you have opened a new shopping mall on the western side of town."

"Dr. Foster in the economics department said that she had talked with you about your expansion plans."

"I understand that you have just received a new study grant from ACW."

3 —Answer the Question "Why Should I See You?"

The work world operates on *value*, not need. You are interesting to a potential employer to the degree that they experience you as being valuable *to them*, not for what you are looking for *from them*. In the body of your cover letter communicate some special way that your skills will be valuable to the potential employer. Create interest in yourself. This will take some basic research in your target field and familiarity with the interests and needs of the specific employer, plus a willingness to show how you can make a difference. Common sense helps.

4 —Use the Language of the Recipient

Every field has its own technology and its accompanying jargon. Use the right terms to indicate your ability and expertise. An excellent way to improve your knowledge of the nomenclature of the field is to read trade journals and articles by professionals in that particular field—see your librarian.

5 —Ask for the Interview

Salespeople call this the "close"—the time when you ask for the business. In this case the "business" is a personal *meeting* (a more subtle word than interview). Ask for it. You can even suggest a date and time.

Susan Montrose Winters
61 Mulberry Place
Wichita, KS 67212
(316) 555-8364
June 3, 1993

Mr. Anthony Ferro, Chairman
Wichita Boys and Girls Club
4216 Canasta Lane
Wichita, KS 67216

Dear Mr. Ferro:

Thank you for telling me about your Board of Directors' decision to connect your older boys and girls to the town beautification objectives. As we discussed, my prior experience with innovative projects, with officials in town government, and with establishing ongoing coordination capability can be very helpful.

Among other things, I have:

- instituted and chaired the UNICEF program for Halloween through church Sunday schools a few years ago;
- established a new auxiliary for the Family Center, to provide a paraprofessional support system to supplement the professionals;
- worked with the business managers of several local organizations to control expenses and evaluate program effectiveness.

I understand that you are interested in someone who can organize your staff and volunteers to coordinate with the Department of Parks and Recreation, in order to develop and implement a new activity and interest for the boys and girls.

It would be a pleasure to respond to a request for a proposal to manage this project. I will call you in four or five days to see if this is desired.

Very truly yours,

Susan Winters

Part Four

Career Counselor Biographies and Directory

The real work for this book was done by the seventy-five individuals whose lives and careers were challenged by the predicaments described in the case histories comprising the central section of this book—and by the twenty-nine highly professional counselors and career coaches who helped them design their strategies and prepare their resumes.

Listed in the following pages are brief biographies and contact information for the counselors. These fine people are known for both the quality of their work and their commitment to people. We salute them and thank them again for the contribution they have made.

Carol Allen is founder and president of Career Agenda, Inc. (560 W. 43rd Street—Suite 40B, New York, NY 10036, 212/268-0564). She has been an outplacement counselor with the Career Development Team, having worked on projects for many major corporations including the New York Life Insurance Company, Dupont de Nemours, Otis Elevator, and AT&T. In Washington, D.C. she served terminally ill individuals and their families as a death-and-dying counselor, and was inspired by Dr. Gerald Jampolsky in formulating and implementing the Healing Heart Program, now the Washington Center for Additudinal Healing. Carol is a member of the American Society of Training and Development.

Jack Ballard is president and co-founder of Third Half of Life Institute, Inc. (93 Cutler Road, Greenwich, CT 06831, 203/661-0015), a nonprofit educational firm designed to help others turn the "bonus years" of postretirement into the most productive and satisfying of their lives. In his earlier career, Jack held managerial positions in the foreign operations of Mobil Oil. He has had extensive training in psychology, counseling, and learning technology.

Phoebe Ballard is vice-president and co-founder of Third Half of Life Institute Inc. Since 1984, when she helped form the company with her husband, Phoebe has been providing transition counseling services to individuals and couples. Phoebe specialized in humanistic/transpersonal psychology as developed by Jung, Rogers, and Assagioli, emphasizing life planning, personal transition management, dream analysis, and psychosynthesis. Phoebe is a member of the International Society of Retirement Planners.

Judy Kaplan Baron is a nationally certified career counselor who has been in private practice (6046 Cornerstone Court West, Suite 208, San Diego, CA 92121, 619/588-7400), since 1978. Judy assists her clients in all facets of career decision-making and job search strategy, including the development of resumes. In addition to career counseling, she is also involved in management consulting and training, which gives her a keen awareness of many different kinds of organizations and the opportunities and hierarchy within them. In addition, she is also a licensed marriage and family counselor, with a significant understanding of how a career impacts other aspects of life. Considered an expert in career development, she has been listed among the valuable resources in the bestselling book, *What Color Is Your Parachute?*, for years.

Joyce Cohen is a management/career consultant who divides her time between Cohen Associates (1088 Black Rock Turnpike, Fairfield, CT 06430, 203/332-7529), and Farren Associates (7353 McWhorter Place, Suite 200, Annandale, VA 22003, 703/256-5712). In her career counseling practice, Joyce's work encompasses consulting with individuals in their career changes, launching new careers, and leading workshops at universities on work trend and job search topics. As a management consultant, Joyce collaborates with Caela Farren in designing programs for career development, preretirement planning, and organizational effectiveness. Joyce has worked closely with over 100 major corporations. She has also published articles in the National Business Employment Weekly, a Wall Street Journal publication.

In 1985, **Patricia Dietze** established Career Workshops (5431 West Roscoe, Chicago, IL 60641, 312/282-6859), a career planning and development service that assists individuals and groups to define their career goals, to identify personal marketing skills, to obtain rewarding positions, and to enhance the quality of their worklife. Patricia's workshops include: career planning and job search, resume writing, interviewing and salary-negotiating skills, balancing home and career, alternative careers for people in the caring professions, sales as a career, and the basics of selling. After teaching for fifteen years, Patricia served for five years as programs coordinator for the Chicago Board of Education. In addition to her university degrees, Patricia has been trained by Richard Bolles, author of *What Color is Your Parachute?*

Barbara Kabcenell Ellman heads Ellman & Associates (7001 Orchard Lake Road, Suite 220B, West Bloomfield, MI 48322, 313/737-7252), a career management organization dedicated to assisting individuals and groups to take control of their worklives. Barbara currently focuses on helping individuals in a twelve-step program, coaching in self-awareness activities, networking, and interviewing/negotiating skills. With twenty years of experience counseling high school, college-age, and adult individuals and groups in their career issues, Barbara's practice is now totally dedicated to career counseling.

Bonnie Traylor-FitzSimmons is a staff manager with US West Communications (P.O. Box 34903, Phoenix, AZ 85067-4903, 602/863-9763). For five years Bonnie was manager of management staffing at Career Resources Centers for US West. Among her many credits, Bonnie has been certified and licensed by Equinox Corporation and Career Development Team to deliver copyrighted career-related programs throughout US West. Bonnie has also designed, written, presented, and trained instructors to deliver five popular US West training programs. In addition, Bonnie conducts individual counseling privately and as a public service within the community.

Monika Freidel is a managing associate with Executive Assets Corporation (411 East Wisconsin Avenue, Suite 990, Milwaukee, WI 53066, 414/271-0505), an individual and group outplacement organization. Currently, Monika divides her time between corporate consulting and advising management in matters of downsizing, plant closings, problem performances, and service delivery. Service delivery includes preparing individuals for the job market from both a psychological and a marketing perspective. For ten years prior to joining Executive Assets, Monika was employed at Wisconsin Bell Telephone, where she developed and directed the company's highly successful corporate outplacement program.

Pam Gross is executive director of CareerMakers (1336 S.W. Bertha Boulevard, Portland, OR 97219, 503/244-1055), a company that offers a very structured, direct, and intense course of study in life planning and job search methodology. In the past eight years, CareerMakers has helped more than 2000 people through job and career transitions. CareerMakers works with individuals facing job loss, those wanting to change careers, and those reentering the job market. Corporations hire CareerMakers to help people whose positions have been terminated because of downsizing, mergers, or buy-outs. CareerMakers even works with high school students, teaching them how to live proactive lives and ultimately find satisfying jobs. Pam is a member of the American Society for Training and Development.

Betsy Jaffe is president of Career Continuum (7 West 14th Street, Suite 20F, New York, NY 10011, 212/675-3926), a consulting firm specializing in career assessment for managers. Her company uses adult development theory, career/life problem solving, action planning, resume preparation, interview rehearsal, and strategic job search marketing plans. Her clients include professionals, managers, executives, and entrepreneurs in all fields from major U.S. corporations to not-for-profit organizations. She was previously director of operations for Catalyst, a nonprofit New York company that promotes women's development, and a senior line manager in retailing for fifteen years. She consults, teaches, and writes on career management issues. In 1991, Dr. Jaffe published *Altered Ambitions, What's Next in Your Life? Winning Strategies to Reshape Your Career* (Donald J. Fine, Inc.).

Eileen Javers is a Career Consultant with OPTIONS, Inc. (215 South Broad Street, 5th Floor, Philadelphia, PA 19107, 215/735-2202), one of the country's first career and human resource consulting services. OPTIONS, Inc. advises individuals on career management, career change, and job search, and consults with organizations on transitions, on-the-job effectiveness, and the impact of social trends on the workplace. They have helped thousands of individuals manage career transitions and develop on-the-job survival strategies.

Michael J. Kenney is a Senior Partner with Career Consultants (107 North Pennsylvania, Suite 400, Indianapolis, IN 46204, 317/264-4171), a human resource consulting firm that offers a broad range of consulting services in six divisions: search, outplacement, testing and assessment, career management, consulting, training, and compensation. Mike has been in the world of career counseling for twenty years, the first ten years as an individual practitioner, the last ten with Career Consultants. He began his professional career as a Roman Catholic priest, and in the mid-seventies moved to Indianapolis where he subsequently began his own independent consulting business. In 1980, Mike entered a partnership with Career Consultants and increased his service base by 1200%!

Clemm Kessler III is owner of Kessler and Associates (6818 Grover Street, Omaha, NE 68106, 402/397-9558), a management and human resources consulting firm offering services in career development, employment and outplacement, organizational development, and strategic change, among other organizational management services. Dr. Kessler was an associate professor of psychology for ten years at the University of Nebraska at Omaha. He left teaching and became director of management development and then vice-president of personnel with the Pacesetters Corporation. In 1980 he established Kessler and Associates. Dr. Kessler holds many distinguished memberships and has been listed in *Who's Who in the Midwest* and *The International Who's Who in Community Service*.

Kathy Kouzmanoff, M.S. is founder and director of Mind's Eye Institute (16445 Audrey Lane, Brookfield, WI 53005, 414/786-1120), which offers personal counseling, workshops, lectures, study groups, and career counseling based on the Myers-Briggs Personality Profile and Richard Bolles' book *What Color is Your Parachute?* Kathy's career counseling can be as brief as three hours, or as long as meeting once weekly for a year. She can take a client deeper to integrate dreams, personal mythology, fantasy, and creative energies, if the client is so inclined. Sometimes a client will create two resumes, one for immediate use and one that will eventually be utilized, but for which the client is not yet ready.

John Mattson is director of Career Services at The Fletcher School, Tufts University (Medford, MA 02155, 617/381-3060). His work includes counseling and workshops in job-search strategies for graduate students in the School of International Relations. In addition, John has a private career counseling firm, Career Crossroads in Concord, Massachusetts, that provides counseling to midlife career changers; he also consults to private schools and other community organizations. John holds an M.Ed. in Counseling from Tufts and a B.A. in Sociology from Boston University. He has also been an executive outplacement counselor and trainer with The Career Development Team in New York City.

Kenton L. McCoy is director of counseling services and coordinator of career planning and placement at Davis and Elkins College (100 Sycamore Street, Elkins, WV 26241, 304/636-1900 x 290). He is responsible for the administration of the campus career and personal counseling services. Most of his time is spent working directly with students and adult clients in career exploration and job search strategy development. He is also a trainer for the Career Development Team, providing internal career development services for numerous Fortune 500 corporations. Ken has been at Davis and Elkins College since 1972, and has completed course work and comprehensive exams for a Ph.D.

Patricia O'Keefe, M.A. is president of Alternatives, a private practice career-counseling firm (350 Cook Street, Denver, CO 80206, 303/393-8747). She counsels clients in all areas of career planning: self-assessment, research, job-search techniques, interviewing, and resume preparation. She has designed and developed a career-counseling process incorporating a thorough action-oriented approach to career decision-making. She has also presented numerous workshops focusing on career decisions, job-search strategies, Myers-Briggs interpretation, resumes, and interviewing techniques. Patricia has been a college instructor and an executive in retail sales. She holds an M.A. in Counseling and Personal Service and a B.A. in Business/Marketing.

William O'Toole is a Ph.D. career consultant/psychologist at Career Strategies, Inc., with offices in Hattiesburg, MS (334 N. 25th Avenue, Suite B, Hattiesburg, MS 39401, 601/544-4561) and Metairie, LA (Two Lakeway Center, 3850 N. Causeway Blvd, Suite 210, Metairie, LA 70002, 504/836-7538). Dr. O'Toole is a licensed psychologist in Mississippi with over ten years' experience in the field of career consultation. His practice offers a broad menu of assistance including anxiety and behavioral difficulties and other personal issues, career/work problems such as combining work and family roles, job-search techniques, coping-with-life demands, and stress reduction. Dr. O'Toole has published several articles and has made numerous presentations at professional organizations on topics related to counseling.

Phyllis Harper Rispoli is principal of her own business, PHR & Associates, a human resources consulting firm in Tempe, Arizona, that has provided training and counseling services to industry and government since 1984. Phyllis's human resources career has spanned more than a decade, during which time she has been a practitioner of training and development, career development, recruitment, and basic skills training. She is a member of the American Society of Training and Development (ASTD), president of the Valley of the Sun Chapter of ASTD, and founding member of the Arizona Career Development Association. PHR & Associates accepts clients through employers only.

Carl Schneider is a career counselor in private practice with Changes (104 Sanborn Avenue, West Roxbury, MA 02132, 617/327-5343). He has also been a psychotherapist since 1978. He subscribes to the life history approach to career counseling that promotes the notion of job-hunters getting positions and even changing careers mainly through a switchboard (network) of friends and specific employers. He once used this personal approach himself to join a new commercial career-counseling firm, Career Directions in Needham, Massachusetts. He was subsequently trained by Richard Germann, a principal in the national outplacement firm, Right Associates. Carl also works part-time at a psychiatric hospital and youth agency.

Jane Shuman, M.A. is a career management consultant and founder of Shuman and Associates (1 South 283 Danby, Villa Park, IL 60181, 708/916-7754). Her company offers services in management development as well as career development. Career services include: coaching on performance issues, development and planning using Benchmarks®, assistance with career choice/career transition decisions, resume preparation, and job-search strategies. In fifteen years as a successful career consultant, Jane has helped more than 5000 people redesign their lives and work. She holds the professional designation of National Certified Counselor. She is also a member of the National Speakers Bureau and the American Society of Training and Development. She is currently on the faculty of Lincoln Land Community College in Springfield, Illinois.

Peggy Simonsen, M.A. is a career development consultant with Career Directions, Inc. (5005 Newport Drive, Suite 404, Rolling Meadow, IL 60008, 708/870-1298). Established in 1979, Career Directions individualizes its approach to meet the specific needs of clients, including testing, career focus, resumes, job-search assistance, and career management strategies. Career Directions also designs corporate career development programs. Peggy is recognized as a leader in the field, with numerous TV and radio credits. She has published *What Can I Do and Who Will Hire Me to Do It?* (Career Directions, 1983); *Getting and Keeping a Job* (Scott Foresman, 1982); and *Becoming a Supervisor* (Scott Foresman, 1982). She has written numerous articles for Career World Magazine and other professional journals.

Alexine Smith is a career counselor/placement officer at Indiana University–Purdue University at Indianapolis (Career and Employment Services, 4464 North Priscilla Avenue, Indianapolis, IN 46226, 317/274-0858). She provides career planning, guidance, and other services to both students and alumni. Alexine also develops written materials and presents workshops related to career planning and development. She recommends and interprets various vocational, occupational, personality, and interest inventories to her clientele. Alexine is also a workshop assistant with the Career Development Team of

Bedford, New York. She serves as a local resource for workshop participants on career-related issues and community-based needs. Her specialty area is resume development. Currently she has a professional resume service and is starting a private practice in career counseling.

Jerry Sturman   is chairman and CEO of The Career Development Team (19 Brookwood Road, Bedford, NY 10506, 914/234-3200), a leading national provider of programs, materials, and consulting in the area of individual and organizational career management. He is a Ph.D. Engineer and his thirty-year career includes faculty positions at MIT and Columbia, partnership in Parsons Brinckerhoff, one of the world's largest engineering firms, and now the top post at CDT. Dr. Sturman is author of *If You Knew Who You Were . . . You Could Be Who You Are,* a comprehensive career-assessment book, and *Managing Your Career with POWER,* a career-management guide for organizational employees (Bierman Publishers, Inc.).

Minh-Nhat Tran   (pronounced Minyet Tran) is a career-development consultant with her own firm (2413 Brickton Road, Wilmington, DE 19803, 302/478-7186). Minh-Nhat established her firm in 1984 for men and women seeking career planning. She saw a need for professionals who had stayed for years in unrewarding jobs because they lacked the techniques of career planning. Minh-Nhat also consults with organizations on design and development of career programs, conducts career-planning workshops, trains other trainers in the delivery of career-development workshops, and consults with managers on employee career-related issues. She holds a master's degree in clinical psychology and has studied with the renowned career-development authority, Richard Bolles.

Melvyn M. Tuggle, Jr.   (president) and **Sharon Tuggle** (vice-president) of Career Concepts Planning Center, Inc. (Centennial Square, 2100 South 7th Street, Suite 255, Rapid City, SD 57701, 605/394-5783, 1-800-456-0832), specialize in career development for professionals. Their firm is the only career-planning company in five states that offers assistance with military conversions, Standard Form 171's, interview training, free lead referrals, company information, career recruiting, personnel management, and human resources development. Their staff includes retired members of the Armed Forces familiar with military–civilian conversions. They advise on local and long-distance job searching, resume writing, personal and family relocation planning, and company and market research.

William D. Young, Ed.D.   is a licensed professional counselor with Career Development Services, Inc. (4823 South Sheridan, Suite 304, Tulsa, OK 74145, 918/665-1162), a firm providing career and vocational counseling to private individuals and corporations. They specialize in mid- and late-career-change issues. They also provide vocational rehabilitation evaluations and expert witness testimony regarding career and vocational issues. Dr. Young has published numerous articles and papers including "Revealing Your Salary" in the National Business Employment Weekly (July 1989). He has also held numerous executive positions in community organizations including the Job Support Center and the Business Advisory Counsel.

In addition we would like to acknowledge the following professionals for submitting excellent material that we were unable to use for this volume:

William R. Heise, L.P.C., N.C.C.C.
Schoolcraft College
18600 Haggerty Road
Livonia, MI 48152-2696

Karen K. Stauffacher
Director of Career Services
University of Wisconsin—Madison
10 Commerce Building
1155 Observatory Drive
Madison, WI 53706

Madeleine T. Swain
President
Swain & Swain, Inc.
405 Lexington Avenue
New York, NY 10174

Ted Risch
11122 E. Gunshot Circle
Tucson, AZ 85749

Susan H. Ogle
15 Old Quarry Road
Woodbridge, CT 06525

Ronald S. Young
Director, Cooperative Education/Job Services
Front Range Community College
3645 West 112th Avenue
Westminster, CO 80030

Further Resources

The number and quality of career and job development books on the market is constantly changing. To get the latest update, contact your local librarian, career counselor or bookseller.

Listed below are other books and career products by Tom Jackson.

BOOKS

The Perfect Job Search (1992)
Doubleday

The Perfect Resume (Second Edition-1990)
Doubleday

Not Just Another Job (1992)
Random House

Guerrilla Tactics in the New Job Market (Second Edition-1991)
Bantam Books

SOFTWARE

The Perfect Resume Computer Kit

Resume Express

The Strategic Letter Writer (Power Letters)

See back page copy for details on this innovative software; or write: Permax Systems, Inc., P.O. Box 6455, Madison, WI 53716-0455; or call toll-free 1-800-233-6460.

THE ULTIMATE GUIDE TO MAKING IT IN TODAY'S JOB MARKET

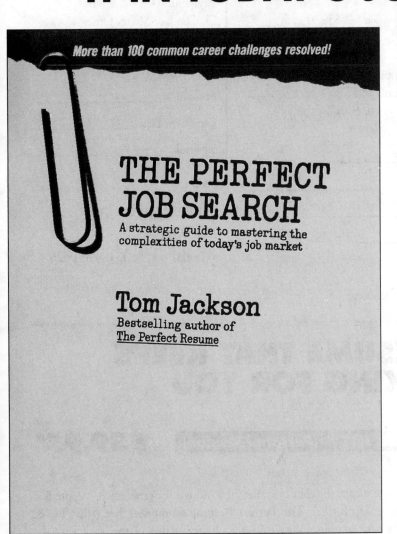

More than 100 common career challenges resolved!

THE PERFECT JOB SEARCH

A strategic guide to mastering the complexities of today's job market

Tom Jackson

Bestselling author of
The Perfect Resume

Bestselling author of **The Perfect Resume** and **Perfect Resume Strategies** and master career strategist Tom Jackson provides the ultimate guide to thriving in today's job market.

Today more than ever, a difficult job market demands impressive, effective strategies that get results! **The Perfect Job Search** combines proven techniques and inspiring advice for job seekers and career changers.

Clearly and consistently presented, this interactive book provides easy access to the six major career dilemmas:

- knowing what you want to do and where to begin
- getting on the fast track—jumping hurdles to success
- creating multiple employer prospects
- writing resumes and cover letters
- taking action to achieve interviews
- turning interviews into offers

This is the one indispensable guide you can't afford to be without!

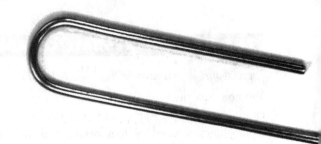

Available at your local bookstore, or if you prefer to order direct, use this coupon form to order.

ISBN	TITLE	PRICE		QTY		TOTAL
18109-4	The Perfect Job Search	$12.50 US	X	_____	=	_____
		$15.50 in Canada	X	_____	=	_____
26745-2	The Perfect Resume, *Revised*	$10.95 US	X	_____	=	_____
		$13.95 in Canada	X	_____	=	_____
		Shipping & Handling (add $2.50 per order)			=	_____
				TOTAL	=	_____

Please send me the title(s) I have indicated above. I am enclosing $ _____.
Send check or money order in U.S. funds (no C.O.D.'s or cash please). Make check payable to
Doubleday Consumer Services. Allow 4-6 weeks for delivery. Prices and availability are subject to change without notice.

NAME_____

ADDRESS_____Apt #_____

CITY_____STATE_____ZIP_____

DR - 9/92

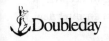 Doubleday

A UNIQUE AND READER-FRIENDLY CATALOGUE OF RESUMES

The ultimate resume catalogue!
An ideal companion to *The Perfect Resume*.

PERFECT RESUME STRATEGIES

Tom Jackson
Author of *The Perfect Resume*

and Ellen Jackson

75 examples of the complete process of self-marketing with the stories behind the documents.

From the author of the bestselling **The Perfect Resume** and **The Perfect Job Search**, comes a unique catalogue of resumes for the job seeker looking for the skills, the insight, and the inspiration so important in today's challenging job market.

Perfect Resume Strategies is a masterful selection of sample resumes gathered from top career counselors across the country that provides an unbeatable resume sampler for the job seeker. The authors analyze each resume by the challenges it addresses, provide strategies for success, and give you examples of self-marketing cover letters and statements.

Especially designed for those readers who find the greatest inspiration in seeing how others have overcome difficulties or who do not like a step-by-step, fill-in-the-blanks format, **Perfect Resume Strategies** is by far the most useful, intelligent, and "reader-friendly" book of any in the field.

This is the one indispensable guide you can't afford to be without!

Or, if you prefer a step-by-step approach to formulating a job-getting resume, **The Perfect Resume,** *Revised* by Tom Jackson is the perfect solution!

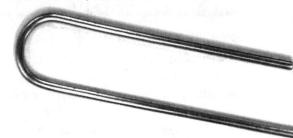

Available at your local bookstore, or if you prefer to order direct, use this coupon form to order.

ISBN	TITLE	PRICE		QTY		TOTAL
18112-4	Perfect Resume Strategies	$12.50 US	X	_____	=	_____
		$15.50 in Canada	X	_____	=	_____
26745-2	The Perfect Resume, *Revised*	$10.95 US	X	_____	=	_____
		$13.95 in Canada	X	_____	=	_____
		Shipping & Handling (add $2.50 per order)			=	_____
			TOTAL		=	_____

Please send me the title(s) I have indicated above. I am enclosing $ _____.
Send check or money order in U.S. funds (no C.O.D.'s or cash please). Make check payable to Doubleday Consumer Services. Allow 4-6 weeks for delivery. Prices and availability are subject to change without notice.

NAME_____

ADDRESS_____Apt #_____

CITY_____STATE_____ZIP_____

DR1 - 9/92

Send completed order form and payment to:
**Doubleday Consumer Services
Dept. DR1
P.O. Box 5071
Des Plaines, IL 60017-5071**

Doubleday

Order Today Toll Free 1-800-233-6460